Hans G. Schütze (Ed.)
Maria Slowey, Alan Wagner, Pierre Paquet

ADULTS
IN HIGHER
EDUCATION

Policies and Practice
in Great Britain and North America

Reports prepared for the Centre for Educational
Research and Innovation of the Organisation for
Economic Co-Operation and Development (OECD)

Almqvist & Wiksell International, Stockholm

ISBN 91-22-00837-3

Almqvist & Wiksell International, Stockholm, 1987

The Organisation for Economic Co-operation and Development (OECD) was set up under a Convention signed in Paris on 14 December 1960, which provides that the OECD shall promote policies designed:

— to achieve the highest sustainable economic growth and employment and a rising standard of living in Member countries, while maintaining financial stability, and thus to contribute to the development of the world economy;

— to contribute to sound economic expansion in Member as well as non-member countries in the process of economic development;

— to contribute to the expansion of world trade on a multilateral, non-discriminatory basis in accordance with international obligations.

The Members of OECD are Australia, Austria, Belgium, Canada, Denmark, Finland, France, the Federal Republic of Germany, Greece, Iceland, Ireland, Italy, Japan, Luxembourg, the Netherlands, New Zealand, Norway, Portugal, Spain, Sweden, Switzerland, Turkey, the United Kingdom and the United States.

The Centre for Educational Research and Innovation was created in June 1968 by the Council of the Organisation for Economic Co-operation and Development for an initial period of three years, with the help of grants from the Ford Foundation and the Royal Dutch Shell Group of Companies. The mandate of the Centre was repeatedly extended by the Council, the present mandate is granted until the end of 1991.

The main objectives of the Centre are as follows:

— *to promote and support the development of research activities in education and undertake such research activities where appropriate;*

— *to promote and support pilot experiments with a view to introducing and testing innovations in the educational system;*

— *to promote the development of co-operation between Member countries in the field of educational research and innovation.*

The Centre functions within the Organisation for Economic Co-operation and Development in accordance with the decisions of the Council of the Organisation, under the authority of the Secretary-General. It is supervised by a Governing Board composed of one national expert in its field of competence from each of the countries participating in its programme of work.

Printed in Sweden by Graphic Systems AB 1987

Table of contents

Preface

Part I.
Hans G. Schütze
NEW FRONTIERS – OLD BARRIERS: Adults in Higher Education.
An Introduction to the Issues 7

Part II.
Maria Slowey
ADULTS IN HIGHER EDUCATION: The Situation in the United
Kingdom 21

Part III.
Alan P. Wagner
ADULTS IN HIGHER EDUCATION: The Situation in the United
States 75

Part IV.
Pierre Paquet
ADULTS IN HIGHER EDUCATION: The Situation in Canada   121

Preface

The purpose of this book is to provide an overview of the situation concerning adult students in higher education in the United States, Canada and Great Britain, to analyse policies and policy options with regard to adult participation, and to offer a number of conclusions about the present situation and future developments. Its origin was a cross-national study conducted under the auspices of the Centre for Educational Research and Innovation (CERI) of the Organisation for Economic Co-operation and Development (OECD), which enquired into the situation of adult students — participation rates, characteristics of adult students (educational and class background, employment and family situon, age, sex and income), as well as organisational and financial policies in these countries as they enhance, or conversely prohibit, adult participation. Although in this study there is an emphasis on adults in degree-awarding programmes, the provision by institutions of higher education of continuing professional education is also dealt with.

Country surveys under the auspices of this project were conducted in eleven countries. Besides the United States, Canada and the United Kingdom, the situation of adult students in Austria, Australia, the Federal Republic of Germany, Finland, France, Ireland, Japan, and Sweden was scrutinised. Some of these country studies have been published separately; for instance, the Swedish study by the publishers of the present volume. The findings of all the country studies have been analysed in a General Report to be published by OECD in Summer 1987.

Like the other country reports, the three country surveys contained in this volume have been drawn up according to a common framework provided by CERI. Besides the analysis of existing information, they also contain entirely new data. The three national reports are preceded by an introductory chapter that draws the surveys together, highlighting the overall issues and providing reference to the situation in other OECD countries.

Maria Slowey, the author of the United Kingdom report, previously a researcher with the Polytechnic of Central London, is presently senior lecturer at the Centre for Continuing Education and Training, Newcastle-upon-Tyne Polytechnic. Alan Wagner is senior research fellow at the School of Education, State University of New York at Albany. Pierre Paquet is the Director of

Research at the Faculty of Continuing Education, University of Montreal. The editor and author of the introductory chapter was the head of the CERI project on Innovation in Higher Education under whose auspices the three country studies have been prepared.

Besides wishing to thank the authors for their diligent work and commitment, the editor would also like to thank Mrs. Carol Chattaway of the United Kingdom Department of Education and Science, Mr. Tim Douglas of the Secretariat of the Canadian Council of Ministers of Education, and the United States Department of Education for the support and encouragement they have given to this project.

Paris, 1st January 1987   Hans G. Schütze

New frontiers – Old barriers: Adults in higher education
An introduction to the issues

by
Hans G. Schütze

The participation of adult students in higher education is one of the issues of growing importance in many developed countries. The phenomenon itself of adult enrolment is not new; in fact, higher education provision for adult students is a long-standing tradition in a number of OECD countries, particularly in North America. However, the topic has emerged as a policy concern not only because of its growing importance in quantitative terms but also as a result of the consequences this increase in adult enrolment entails for the provision of higher education, the contents of curricula, and methods of teaching.

Although there are considerable variations among the industrialised countries, it is fair to say that in most of them adults are becoming, or already have become, an important "new group" in universities, polytechnics and colleges. Previously, even in the few institutions having a tradition of academic provision for these students, adult participation was always marginal, limited to non-degree studies through short courses administered by extra-mural or external

7

departments. But now adult participation has transgressed the boundaries of extra-mural studies and is moving from the margin into the centre of the university's mission. Thus, adults are not merely another new minority group but rather, both in terms of number and importance, are already a major part of the higher education population in some countries, and will soon be in most others.

However important the non-traditional age group has become in terms of demand, real or potential, for higher education, relatively little is known about this new clientele. Likewise, although there is a wide variety of responses to this demand, both on the part of institutions and policy-makers at the various levels concerned, little coherent information is available about the essential issues underlying adult participation. What are the educational needs of adults? What is their preferred mode of study? How do adults learn? How do they learn best? What are the principal factors that motivate adults to return to higher education, or to enrol for the first time? What are the main barriers they face? Which policies and institutional practices enhance adult participation and conversely, which ones present obstacles that adults cannot overcome without difficulty? What are the actual characteristics of the adults who do enrol, and how do they compare with those of identified target groups (in cases where explicit policies designed to promote adult education exist)? What is the impact, if any, of higher education studies on the professional career and personal development of those who have participated?

Questions like these were at the origin of the study for which the following reports on the United Kingdom, the United States and Canada were prepared. Not all of them could be answered by the country surveys, let alone provide the basis for cross-country comparisons. This is not only due to important variations from one country to another, both regarding higher education systems and approaches to non-traditional students, but also to a lack of reliable and comparable statistical data. But the authors of the country reports contained in this volume have done some genuine detective work by putting together and interpreting data from various sources and, in the case of the United Kingdom report, collecting new data that help to illuminate what has been largely a dark field or, at best, a grey zone.

In the following, a brief summary of the issues will be given which is intended to facilitate the understanding of the context and the particular features of the systems in the three countries. In the first section, particular developments and features of the United Kingdom, the United States, and Canada will be discussed and the respective roles that higher education and non-academic adult education play in responding to demand from adults. The second section focuses on traditional obstacles that have kept adults from enrolling as well as new frontiers that are being conquered in overcoming the barriers of time and distance. A final section will briefly review the main findings and conclusions of the OECD study as a whole of which the three country reports have been a part.

I. ADULT DEMAND AND THE ROLE OF
HIGHER EDUCATION

Adult demand for education and training is not addressed exclusively to higher education. Educational opportunities for adults are provided by a variety of institutions and professional associations, in settings ranging from voluntary organisations, churches, trade unions, employers' associations, libraries or museums, or broadcasting media, to public and private schools, colleges and universities. Programmes take a multiplicity of forms, such as classroom tuition, workshops, conferences, seminars, television or radio courses, guided yet mostly self-directed learning programmes, demonstrations, excursions and the like. The exact shape and importance of higher education in this colourful mosaic of opportunities cannot be easily determined since the role of higher education varies considerably from country to country. It is dependent on the overall structure of this sector and the specific functions it has been assigned or assumed as well as on the availability of other, non-academic provision that is specifically geared to, or suitable for, adult needs.

Examples of such non-academic institutions catering to adult learners include, for example, the *Volkshochschulen* (i.e. Adult Education Colleges) in the German-speaking countries, which have their equivalent in Scandinavia, or the Technical and Further Education (TAFE) sector in Australia. In the case of Germany, the community-based *Volkshochschul*-sector provides some 8 million students annually with adult education courses that can lead to upper secondary school-leaving certificates or other non-academic diplomas but commonly do not lead to awards. Their existence is one of the principal reasons why universities and *Fachhochschulen* (polytechnics) play only a minor role in providing education for adults. Thus, about eight times as many adults enrol in adult education colleges as compared with total enrolment in higher education degree programmes. About the same ratio is found in the case of Sweden where more than six times as many people are enrolled in study circles than participate in higher education (1).

The size and importance of these non-academic adult education sectors are even greater when not only Adult Education colleges and Study Circles but all the many other providers of adult education are taken into account. Thus, enterprises and trade unions, public radio and TV, the Chambers of Crafts and of Industry and Commerce, as well as a number of commercial providers, offer a wide variety of vocational and non-vocational courses for adults. Although it is virtually impossible to ascertain the total number of people participating in their programmes — due to the scarcity of coherent data and the problem of double counting — it is clear that the great majority of adult education opportunities in these above-mentioned countries is not offered by the formal sector, i.e. general and vocational schools or higher education institutions, but by a highly diversified, non-formal, adult education sector.

This applies even to university-level professional continuing education, i.e.

refresher and up-dating courses for professional groups such as physicians, lawyers, teachers, civil engineers, and architects who already hold first (or further) higher education degrees. According to a series of recent studies in Germany, only 5.8 per cent of such courses were provided by higher education institutions, with the remainder the domain of bodies such as professional associations, Chambers, and specialised institutions outside the regular higher education system (2).

This overall picture of a university-type higher education sector which is relatively little involved in adult education also applies to most other European countries, and to Australia, New Zealand and Japan where a variety of other institutions and bodies cater for adult demand. In quantitative terms, this is even true for the United Kingdom where universities have a long-standing tradition of extra-mural provision for adults, a tradition which the more recent polytechnics have followed. Thus, while the number of adults engaged annually in adult education in England and Wales has been estimated to be around 6 million annually (representing about 16 per cent of the adult population), only 385 000 were enrolled in universities, some 230 000 of whom in extra-mural departments (3). Although this number compares well to, for instance, Japan, where only 150 000 students are enrolled in the University Extension Programmes and university Learning Centres (4), it represents only a small fraction of the total adult population engaged in continuing education activities.

The picture is different in North America where universities and colleges play a much more significant role in providing for adult learners. This is true with respect both to degree and to non-degree studies. Two-year Junior and Community Colleges, in particular, offer a wide variety of vocationally-oriented and general education courses, many of which can be taken either for credit, leading to a (two-year) associate or a (four-year) bachelor degree, or as non-credit courses. According to a recent survey in Canada, the majority of adult learners were enrolled in community colleges and in universities (34 and 22 per cent respectively), while other public institutions, such as school boards, voluntary organisations, employers and unions account for the rest (5). In the United States, according to Wagner's country survey in this volume, 33 million adults 25 years of age and older participated in organised post-high school learning activities in 1983. Of these, approximately 6 million received instruction through programmes offered by institutions of higher education.

These North American examples reflect a long-standing tradition in these countries of serving adults both through extension departments and in regular programmes offered by colleges and university-level professional departments and schools. The contrast between North American and European universities in their educational provision for adults mirrors differences in the more general concepts and roles of higher education held in these continents. Much of the Continental European tradition was built around the Humboldt concept of universities as primarily research institutions and hence emphasis was given to scientific research and the combination of research and post-graduate teaching. Under the influence of this model, access to higher education was, by and large, restricted to a selected élite, and only recently have higher education institutions opened their doors to larger numbers of students from a wider variety of social backgrounds. In North America, while the share of older and more prestigious universities initially followed the European pattern, the majority of institutions, starting with the land-grant colleges, were built on the idea of a university as a service agency for the whole community.

This latter concept implied two consequences: first, that the curriculum was to be democratised to serve not so much (or not only) a relatively small élite but to provide broad, liberal, and practical education for the community at large; second, that higher education institutions were to respond to demand from various groups in the community including adults.

This brief categorisation of the different traditions of higher education in (Continental) Europe and North America is, of course, over-simplified and neglects a number of other important differences. But this categorisation is useful in explaining the variations apparent in the way adults are, or are not, participating in higher education in different countries. In other words, adult education and higher education have different roles and relationships depending on the size and importance of the non-academic adult education sector which in turn depends on the accessibility and curriculum of the higher education sector. In countries such as Germany, where university-based education was reserved for would-be researchers or professionals in a limited number of academic occupations, a well-developed non-academic adult education sector has been serving all those excluded from the holy grail of higher studies. By contrast, in countries such as the United States, the education of adults has been conceived as part of the mission of higher education and while other non-academic providers have played, and continue to play, the leading role, universities and colleges have an established place in serving adult students. In saying this, it is not being suggested that higher education in these countries has fully adapted their curricula or modes of delivery to the adult student; in fact, some experts argue that higher education provision for adults in the United States is still marginal compared to that for the traditional age groups:

> "Most colleges and universities continue to serve mainly the traditional 18 to 21 year-old student population. Even at Community Colleges, older adults attend mainly in the evenings and are taught mostly by part-time faculty with little allegiance to basic institutional goals.
>
> Likewise, at public four-year colleges, the average age of students is increasing; yet professors are accustomed to teaching youths and are reluctant, often for career advancement reasons, to teach adult classes. At most selective universities and independent colleges, the move to accommodate older students has been slow or non-existent" (6).

However dominant the group of traditional-age students in higher education may still be, evidence from the country surveys and other sources suggests that the situation in almost all the OECD countries is gradually changing. Although it may be too early in many places to speak of the "greying of the campus" (7) or the "adultification of higher education" (8), a variety of policies have recently been put in place that have enhanced, and will further enhance, adult participation. Furthermore, many institutions have started to respond on their own and to cater to adult demand without the impetus of specific policies.

Not all the growing adult demand for education and training will flow into the mills of higher education, and non-academic adult education providers will continue to play an important role. In fact, the latter have a number of advantages over traditional higher education institutions — frequently dense geographical networks, faculties consisting mainly of practitioners, curricula and attendance options suited to adult needs, and lower psychological barriers to access in the case of would-be learners with poor educational backgrounds. On the other hand, higher education establishments are relatively well placed to respond to the varied needs of the groups of adult students identified above, not only because they generally have highly-trained teachers, advanced technological equipment and other learning facilities, but because they enjoy the attraction of academic prestige. To assume a greater role in serving adults, however, will make it necessary for higher education not only to design courses and programmes in such a way as to make them relevant to adult needs and interests but also to search for new schedules and forms of delivery that are compatible with work and family situations and adult modes of learning.

II. OLD BARRIERS — NEW FRONTIERS

Although demand for education and training from adults is growing, many establishments of higher education are little prepared to adapt to adult demand by making adequate provision that responds to the educational needs and specific circumstances of adults. In fact, there is evidence that under the prevailing conditions, many are actually barred from access. Such barriers have been widely discussed (9) and have been usefully classified as "dispositional" (relating to attitude and self-perception of the adult learner, especially those of only limited educational background), "institutional" (referring, for example, to lack of suitable courses, inconvenient schedules or locations, or high fees), and "situational" (e.g. lack of time for study due to work, family or other social responsibilities, lack of financial support, means of transportation, child care facilities, etc.) (10).

Available research in most OECD countries shows that these barriers affect a large number of would-be learners. Prominent among the reasons given by adults for not enrolling in (higher) education are lack of time and money. Although these reasons are certainly plausible and may apply in many cases, it has been noted that they are also more socially acceptable than others, such as lack of self-confidence, or of ability or interest and this may help to explain why

12

they are more frequently cited. Besides "too busy" and "can't afford it", other frequently-cited reasons are lack of information, unavailability of suitable courses, geographical barriers, and lack of entry qualifications. Obviously, there are marked differences in the significance of these obstacles depending on the preferred mode of study and also on the sex of the would-be student, women being particularly affected by family responsibilities.

As mentioned above, situational and institutional barriers — important as they are — may not be the most critical ones. Perhaps the major barrier remains one of attitude, not only of would-be students, but also of others in their environment and of society in general. At its base lies the assumption — still widespread, although gradually losing its importance — that education, including higher education, is only for the young as preparation for adult life (11). This tends to be most deeply entrenched among adults whose initial education was poor and who have never come back to any form of continuing education. But even among those who, because of their efforts and success in initial or continuing education, aspire to enrol in higher education courses, the fear of being too old to learn and the fear that their knowledge is obsolete may act as powerful disincentives. This may affect, for example, women wishing to return to professional life after raising a family or older professionals whose field has been seriously altered by scientific research, modern technologies or new patterns of work organisation.

Of equal importance is the fact that although recurrent patterns of learning over a lifetime are increasingly common, hiring and career patterns have not yet been adapted and still favour the "front-end" model of education and training (12). On the other hand, more employers are now aware of the need for updating and enlarging the skills and competencies of their workforce, including the highly trained, and they often encourage or even require participation in re-training and updating programmes offered by educational institutions from some members of their personnel (13).

But even for those adults who have overcome these attitudinal or dispositional barriers, the remaining obstacles to access are still formidable. Although institutional barriers that are geographical, financial and structural have often been lowered by a variety of innovative policies and practices, especially in North America, many would-be learners continue to be deterred. The same is true of situational barriers, i.e. those connected with adults' daily lives. Indeed, lack of child-care facilities figures prominently on the list of reasons women in particular give for their non-participation — an obstacle that is almost as high as lack of finance.

Although many of the traditional barriers to adult participation in higher education are still in place, some have been eliminated and others considerably reduced in importance. Policies and institutions themselves have begun to break down some of the walls around the traditional university and to build bridges over the moats that have barred most non-traditional students from access in the past. Especially in the United States and Canada, a number of

13

new policies and innovative institutional practices have greatly facilitated the participation of adults. Open admission schemes or the recognition of work experience as a substitute for academic entry qualifications, part-time modes of study, credit transfer and improved counselling and information services are examples.

Finance remains a major obstacle. With the exception of the United Kingdom, where specific "mature student" awards exist, there are no specific financial provisions for adult students as such. Evidence suggests that student support, to the extent that adults are eligible at all, tends to be neither sufficient, given the special needs of adults, nor suited to the specific modes by which most of them participate in degree programmes. This applies in particular to the non-eligibility of part-time studies under most finance systems, although in the United States and Canada, recent amendments to a number of loan-awarding support schemes have included part-time studies, if only on a very limited scale.

While the financial hurdle remains a serious problem, big steps have been made in overcoming barriers of time and distance. Learning at a distance, independent of campus or classroom attendance and of schedules set up to serve full-time students, is particularly appropriate for adults who have to combine studies with the other pressing demands of work, family and social commitments. Single purpose distance teaching universities and distance provision by traditional institutions have played an increasing role in providing second chance opportunities for adults (14).

But in spite of the development of new information and telecommunication technologies, distance education has relied so far mainly on more traditional media, mostly print, though also television, radio, telephone and audio-cassettes. Even the latter, however, have been chiefly used to supplement and support printed course materials. Newer distance universities that have gone into operation only recently, such as the Dutch Open University and the Japanese University of the Air, have also followed this general pattern.

In contrast to the relatively cautious attitude of the European and the Japanese institutions, new information and telecommunication technologies seem to be more enthusiastically embraced in North America, particularly the United States, where a growing number of institutions, or consortia of institutions, have been in the process of replacing classroom tuition and textbooks with interactive electronic media.

With TV, radio, and telephones now commonplace in most households in OECD countries and the presence of satellite and cable TV, video recorders and home computers spreading rapidly over the last few years, there is a growing base for the increased use of these technologies for educational purposes. This raises a host of policy issues and practical questions that must be taken into account when attempting to assess potential adult participation in higher education: How can adults be reached and motivated to learn and can technology enhance this process? Can computerised counselling and guidance services help those not familiar with the education system to find out about the post-secondary opportunities available and which programmes are suited to their perceived needs or aspirations? To what extent are information and telecommunication technologies suited to adult learning needs? Is the self-controlled and paced or independent learning methods using new technologies suited to the particular ways adults learn? To what extent do they need a social environment or individual help in order to pursue their studies successfully? Obviously, general answers cannot be given to those questions that depend on the type of adult learner, his or her motivation and objectives as well as the nature of the programme chosen.

While many questions are outstanding, it is clear that sophisticated, interactive educational technologies can indeed bridge the barriers of time and distance, which have been most powerful in keeping adult students from entering higher education. Yet, the same technologies may be erecting new obstacles for adults that are just as powerful.

The most important of these obstacles is the high cost of advanced equipment which can put such technologies out of the reach of would-be students from lower-income groups. With educational institutions relying increasingly on more costly technologies, those who can afford home computers, multiple cable television services, video cassette recorders and the like will have access to a much wider choice of educational options than those who cannot afford them. This raises the issue of equity, and concerns have been voiced that we run the risk of creating not only a society of information "haves" and "have nots", but also of education "haves" and "have nots" (15). A second obstacle may be seen in the frequent lack of familiarity of older adults with more sophisticated, especially interactive, technologies. Older peoples will probably be thus less motivated to engage in educational programmes that use them.

It must be noted, however, that the interest in, and expansion of, new information and telecommunication media are not limited to higher education institutions or departments specialising in distance learning. Increasingly, post-secondary institutions serving students on campus use computer work stations and some of them are either supplying their students with micro-computers or requesting them to bring their own. The introduction of such technologies is often done in close co-operation with industry — many hardware producers have discovered that higher education holds the promise of an enormous market for their products.

Thus, while the introduction of the new media has a special importance for adult students, it is affecting higher education as a whole. Although many of the implications of this development — for the institutions, the entire pedagogical process of teaching and learning, the organisation of research — are far from clear, it is probably not an overstatement to predict that new educational technologies will not only change the mode of delivery but also the entire organisation of scientific research and training.

The following three country surveys will deal more specifically with the issues raised above and give an account of public policies and institutional practices, of innovations and longer – term developments, of barriers and incentives to a greater participation by adults – as they are seen to prevail in the United Kingdom, the United States and Canada. In the concluding section of this introduction we shall attempt to do exactly the opposite, namely to give a bird's view of the overall situation and developments in the Western industrialized countries – as they have emerged from the OECD study.

III. ADULTS IN HIGHER EDUCATION – FIFTEEN SUMMARY THESES [16]

(1) Higher education is traditionally characterised by classroom teaching, full-time attendance and a student body consisting of young people aged between 18 and 25 years with normal academic entry qualifications. This traditional pattern is undergoing gradual, yet radical change in most industrialised countries. While classroom teaching, full-time courses, and students of the traditional age group are still dominant, off-campus provision and independent learning, part-time study and adult students are clearly and steadily on the increase.

(2) There are several factors behind the increase in adult participation in higher education. Most important among these is probably the recurrent need to refresh and enlarge work-related skills and knowledge, made necessary by accelerated technological and social change. Other factors of a socio-economic nature include increased opportunities, and frequently the need for career changes in mid-life, greater non-work time due to shorter working hours, longer periods of retirement and of time out of work forced upon the individual by unemployment, and the higher levels of initial education that are conducive to continuing interest in education.

(3) Perhaps the most influential element behind the increase in adult demand for higher education (and for education generally) goes beyond these factors to embrace a concern with larger quality-of-life issues. Increasingly, there is general recognition of an individual right to personal growth and development which is partly achieved through education, and the accompanying realisation that education is not a process which is confined to a person's youth. Rather, like personal growth and development, it is a life-time affair.

(4) In line with these different factors, four categories of adult students can be distinguished:
   – Those who enter or re-enter higher education as adults in order to pursue mainstream studies leading to a full first degree or diploma ("delayers", "deferrers", or those who are admitted on credentials for work experience or via second-chance educational routes);
   – Those who re-enter to update their professional knowledge, or seek to acquire additional qualifications, in order to change occupation or ad-

vance in their career ("refreshers", "recyclers");

— Those without previous experience in higher education who enrol for professional purposes especially in courses of short duration, though the boundaries between the "professional" and "general" may often not be very clear (e.g. in languages or computer sciences);

— Those, with or without previous experience in higher education, who enrol for courses with the explicit purpose of personal fulfilment.

(5) Comparing adults with their younger fellow students, the former face a number of specific obstacles, particularly when they consider studying for a degree. Most of these have to do with the student's life situation, i.e. work and family obligations, and, generally speaking, higher education institutions have not yet adapted their entry requirements, curricula, schedules, modes of delivery, and support services to the needs of this new clientele. These difficulties can often not be addressed at the level of individual institutions since in many countries questions such as access requirements, modes of study, and student aid are regulated by law.

(6) Organisational policies and practices thus play a critical role in that they can perpetuate or, conversely, eliminate or lower outstanding barriers to adult participation in degree studies. Open admission or recognition of work or life experience as an equivalent to academic entry qualifications represent examples of the latter. Of even greater importance is the availability of part-time modes of study that permit the adult student to combine education and work. Other examples of innovative organisational options that facilitate adult participation include distance study, credit transfer, modular courses and the availability of suitable information and counselling facilities.

(7) Another eminently important factor is money. While finance is important for all students, it is particularly crucial for adults who must find the means of meeting not only the costs of study and their own maintenance but also that of their families. Three general patterns for student aid to adults can be distinguished:

— Specific support schemes for adult students that take account of, and make special provision for, their socio-economic situation;

— Student support schemes that are "neutral" in the sense that they apply equally to traditional-age and adult students without making special allowance for the specific needs of older students;

— Student aid schemes that actually discriminate against adult students in various ways, ranging from upper age ceilings for study support to the non-eligibility of part-time students for financial aid.

The first category must be considered exceptional and most types of financial support fall into the latter two categories. On the whole, student support for which adults are eligible is neither sufficient, given their specific needs, nor suited to the modes by which most adults tend to participate in degree programmes. This is exemplified by the non-eligibility of distance and part-time programmes for support in most countries.

(8) Participation by adults in degree programmes varies significantly from country to country depending largely on the existence of explicit policies in favour of adult enrolment, and institutional responses to this source of demand such as flexible organisational policies, open admission rules, and part-time provision. Accordingly, adult participation is high in Sweden and the United States, in the former case because of explicit policies, in the latter due to a flexible, market-oriented approach in higher education. Participation is low (under 10 per cent) in countries such as France, Germany, Austria and Japan, whose systems are highly structured and relatively inflexible.

(9) Although adults are a highly diversified group, there are some dominant characteristics of adult students who enrol in degree programmes. In all the countries surveyed in the framework of the CERI study, they tend to be relatively young, the large majority being between 25 (the minimum age fixed for the purpose of defining adult students in this study) and 35 years old. While in the United States, Sweden and Finland, women represent the majority among adult students, in the other countries women are somewhat under-represented though their share is increasing. As to educational background, the majority of older adult students possess a higher level of initial education than the adult population generally. And, as is true for traditional-age students in higher education, students with working class backgrounds are under-represented in relation to the total population, although to a lesser degree than their younger counterparts. As might be expected, the large majority of adult students are in some form of paid employment and are married, many of them with children. Altogether, then, while the majority of adult students do not differ significantly from younger ones in terms of their class and educational backgrounds, they do so in terms of their life situation where they share characteristics typical of their non-student peer group (regarding employment, marriage, children, etc.).

(10) The increase of adult participation has occurred to a lesser extent in degree studies, and most older students pursue some form of continuing education, i.e. shorter non-degree courses. While some countries have a long-standing tradition of extra-mural provision, in others universities are scarcely engaged in continuing education, leaving the task to the non-academic adult education sector. In all countries, however, policies have been developed recently to promote continuing education through higher education, both at the governmental and institutional level.

(11) In the past, the emphasis of university-provided continuing education was on the liberal arts; now professional continuing education emerges as a field of particular visibility and importance. Behind this lies the recognition that the speed of change in science and technology has become such that universities and other comparable institutions can no longer claim to provide their young graduates with the skills and knowledge sufficient for their whole professional life. While, in the past, professional associations and other institutions outside higher education provided the bulk of refresher or updating

courses, increasingly the higher education sector is assuming these tasks.

(12) Judging from recent developments in policies and practices, continuing education, professional and otherwise, is no longer considered a marginal activity of higher education. Rather, policy makers and institutions alike have come to regard continuing education as an important mission of universities and other higher education institutions comparable to their two other principal missions, namely research and the teaching of young under-graduate students.

(13) In the past, time and distance have been major obstacles to the participation of adult students. While study by correspondence or broadcast were designed to overcome these, the actual significance of distance education remained marginal. The development of new telecommunication and information media which permit interactive modes of communication between teacher and learner are bringing about what many experts see as a turning point in the role of distance teaching and learning. To realise the full potential of the new technologies, however, a number of areas need to be addressed, in particular the development of suitable courseware.

(14) New technologies, while removing some of the barriers to adult participation, might erect new ones that are equally difficult to overcome. One of these is the cost of the more sophisticated information and telecommunication equipment — multiple cable television services, video cassette recorders, video disc playback machines, home computers — which may put such technology, and hence education, out of reach of many would-be students, particularly those from low-income backgrounds.

(15) The participation of adults in higher education in increasing numbers, their gradual integration into mainstream provision, and the growing recognition of continuing education as a genuine mission of higher education, of equal importance and status to research and initial education, typify many of the innovations in higher education as a whole.

NOTES AND REFERENCES

1. Abrahamson, K. (1986), *Adult Participation in Swedish Higher Education: A Study of Organisational Structures, Educational Designs and Current Policies,* Stockholm (Almqvist & Wiksell).
2. Allesch, J. *et al.* (1983), *Berufsbezogene wissenschaftliche Weiterbildung an den Hochschulen — Perspektiven und Modelle* (Professional Continuing Education through University Level Higher Education Institutions — Perspectives and Patterns), Bonn (Federal Ministry of Education and Science).
3. Advisory Council for Adult and Continuing Education (ACACE) (1982), *Continuing Education — From Policies to Practice,* Leicester, pp. 42 and 46.
4. Yano, M. (1986) *Adult Learning in Japanese Higher Education — A Consideration of the Economic Aspects,* in: F. Klingler/P. Posch (eds), Studierende mit Berufserfahrung (Adult Students with Work Experience), Vienna

(Böhlau) 1986, p. 77—96.

5. Canadian Association for Adult Education/Institut canadien d'éducation des adultes (CAAE/ICEA), *op. cit.*, p. 21. Note that the respective share of part-time enrolment in: Secretary of State, *One Person Out of Five*, Ottawa, 1984, is 28 per cent only, which indicates that the CAAE/ICEA figures might be somewhat overstated. Cf. also Paquet, in this volume.

6. Peterson, R. (1981), "Opportunities for Adult Learners", in: A. Chickering et al. (Eds.), *The Modern American College*, San Francisco (Jossey Bass).

7. Weinstock, R. (1978), *The Greying of the Campus*, New York (Educational Facilities Laboratory).

8. Abrahamson, K. *op. cit.*

9. Cf. OECD (1979), Learning Opportunities for Adults, Vol. III (The Non-Participation Issue), Paris; H G Schützel D. Istance, *Recurrent Education Revisited: Patterns of Participation and Finance*, Stockholm (Almquist & Wiksell) 1987; Advisory Council for Adult and Continuing Education (ACACE), op. cit.
   See further Rubenson, K. (1986), "Participation of Adults in Education: Old and New Barriers", in: Wagner, A./Lynton, E. (Eds.) *Technology and the Adult Learner: Widening Access or Erecting New Barriers.*, 1987 (forthcoming).

10. Following Cross, Patricia (1981), *Adults as Learners*, San Francisco (Jossey Bass).

11. ACACE, *op cit.*, p. 66.

12. Levin, H./Schütze, H. G. (1983), "Economic and Political Dimensions of Recurrent Education", in: Levin, H./Schütze, H. G. (Eds.), *Financing Recurrent Education — Strategies for Increasing Employment, Job Opportunities and Productivity*, Beverly Hills (Sage).

13. Levin, H./Schütze, H. G. (1984), op.cit.; see also Lynton, E. (1984) *The Missing Connection Between Business and Universities*, New York (MacMillan).

14. For details see OECD/CERI (1987), *Adults in Higher Education, Paris (forthcoming)*.

15. Lewis, R. (1983), *Meeting Learners Needs through Telecommunications — A Directory and Guide to Programs*, Washington, D.C. (Centre for Learning and Telecommunications).

16. OECD/CERI (1987) *op. cit.*

Adults in higher education:
The situation in the United Kingdom

by
Maria Slowey

TABLE OF CONTENTS

	Page
Chapter I: Adult Students on Degree Level Courses	25
A. Background: The Higher Education System	25
1. Introduction	25
2. Admission to First Degree Courses	29
3. Structure of Degree Courses	30
4. Funding of Higher Education Institutions	30
5. Voluntary-Aided and Direct Grant Colleges	31
6. Financing Fees and Maintenance Costs	31
B. Characteristics of Mature Students in Higher Education	31
C. Policies and Practice of Institutions of Higher Education Concerning Adult Students	38
1. Admissions	38
2. Credit Transfer	41
3. Attendance Options	43
4. Information and Counselling Services for Adults	43
D. Modes of Financing for Mature Age Students	47
E. Evaluation of Adult Participation in Full (First) Degree Programmes	49
1. Attitudes of Policy Makers	49
2. Attitudes of Institutions	50
3. Attitudes of Employers	50
4. Effects of undertaking degree studies on later economic position	51
Chapter II: Continuing Education	53
A. Background to Continuing Education	53
1. Introduction	53
2. Local Education Authority Provision	54
3. Universities and Responsible Bodies	55
4. Residential Colleges	55
5. Open University	55
6. Manpower Services Commission/Training Services Division	56
7. Broadcasting	56
8. Other Sources of Continuing Education	57
9. Employers' Involvement in Continuing Education	57
10. Summary	61
B. Characteristics of Students on Continuing Education Programmes	61

  Page

C. Continuing Education: Programmes and Policies of
    Universities, Polytechnics and the Open University   64
        1. Universities   64
        2. Polytechnics   65
        3. Open University   66
D. Costs and Financing of Continuing Education Courses   67
        1. Expenditure   67
        2. Fees   67
Conclusions   68
    Abbreviations   69
    Notes and References   70
    Appendices   71

Chapter I
Adult students on degree level courses

A. BACKGROUND: THE HIGHER EDUCATION SYSTEM

1. *Introduction*

Nineteen eighty-four saw the publication in the United Kingdom of two major national policy documents on continuing education. Covering the university sector of higher education was the report of the working party on continuing education of the University Grants Committee (UGC), while covering public sector higher education was the report of the working party of the National Advisory Body for Public Sector Higher Education (NAB) (1). (Hereafter these will be referred to as the UGC and NAB reports respectively). These reports clearly highlighted the importance which policy makers place on continuing education and the unique contribution which they see higher education as making to its development. In referring to the traditional role of universities in serving the advancement of knowledge by teaching and research, the UGC report argues the case for regarding continuing education as an increasingly important vehicle for dissemination of knowledge. The report makes its position clear by the recommendation that, while acknowledging the academic, organisational and financial problems to be overcome,

> "... the stated policy of universities should be to regard education as a central part of their role and to give it the status and recognition equal to research, and to the traditional teaching of young undergraduates". (UGC, p. 7)

The NAB report makes similar exhortations to institutions of higher education in the public sector.

25

"The positive approach that is needed must exist at all levels of the institution but the responsibility rests at the top with the institutional leadership. Commitments to continuing education must be demonstrated by making it a major function of the institution on a par with its commitments to initial education and, where appropriate, to research". (NAB, p. 31)

In addition to both reports making the case for regarding continuing education as an integral function of institutions of higher education, thus moving it from the periphery to the centre, both reports adopted extremely broad definitions of what they included within the term "continuing education"; the UGC, for example, defined continuing education as:

". . . any form of education, whether vocational or general, resumed after an interval following the end of continuous initial education". (UGC, p. 1)

Four particular categories were identified as coming within this definition. Firstly, adults on full-time courses, i.e. those starting undergraduate courses at age 21 or over, and post-graduate courses at age 25 or over. Secondly, part-time degree and diploma courses. Thirdly, extra-mural courses of a general liberal adult education nature. Fourthly, post-experience vocational education courses (PEVE). While, as will be seen below, public sector institutions of higher education differ significantly in terms of their provision for adults in these categories (in particular the significantly greater opportunities they provide for part-time study options on degree and diploma courses) the NAB report adopted a similarly broad concept of continuing education, bringing within its compass

". . . not only those attending short courses for post-experience vocational education or other objectives, but the many mature students attending longer degree and non-degree courses leading to a qualification". (NAB, p. 1)

There has been some debate as to whether the use of such a broad definition results in a loss of meaning for the term. Overall however the argument is for greater flexibility in higher education in relation, for example, to issues such as attendance options, admissions criteria, and accreditation. Perhaps the NAB report summarises the position most clearly by pointing out that *continuing education is best defined by the articulated needs of adult students rather than by the characteristics of courses.* An adult may therefore regard an under-graduate degree course on the one hand, or a short non-qualifying course on the other hand, as constituting the best way for them to meet their own particular continuing education requirements.

In attempting to map out the pattern and characteristics of mature student participation in higher education in Britain, there are three problems relating to definitions and the way in which statistics are collected which means that directly comparable data is not always available. In the first place, official statistics are collected, and usually presented, separately for England and Wales, Scotland and Northern Ireland. The second problem relates to the definition of what constitutes a "mature student". For some official purposes

26

(for example, grants awards) the age selected is 25, whereas for other purposes (for example, the Open University entry requirements prior to 1985) the lower age limit may be 21. As far as possible, we have used the age of 25; however, although it may be slightly confusing to present data based on different regions and different ages, in some cases this is all that is available and it seems preferable to leaving gaps in the information. The basis on which information is presented will be indicated clearly in the text.

The third problem relates to the definition of higher education. In the U.K., the term "higher education" usually refers to all advanced courses provided in universities, the Open University, polytechnics and other maintained, grant-aided, or assisted further education institutions. In England and Wales, there are 34 universities, 30 polytechnics, and over 500 colleges of further education [90 per cent of the courses in about 70 of the latter were estimated to be of an advanced nature (2)]. Advanced courses are broadly those which lead to qualifications of a higher standard than the highest school leaving certificate or General Certificate in Education Advanced Level or its equivalent. This is actually a broader definition than that suggested for purposes of the CERI/OECD study and means that many professional courses and sub-degree qualifications are included in the statistics. In Section B, the data from a national survey of mature students is re-analysed using the definitions suggested for this study, but in this introduction population figures are given even where they do not strictly comply with the definition of degree equivalent courses.

As Table 1 shows, it is estimated that in the U. K. in the academic year 1983-84, there were about 284 000 students aged 25 or over attending courses of an advanced nature (as defined above) in universities, the Open University, polytechnics and other public sector institutions. This figure represented about 32 per cent of the total student population, but for a variety of reasons this is an overestimate of mature students on degree level courses. Firstly, it includes all students, many of whom were continuing courses started at a younger age. Secondly, it includes those on post-graduate courses. Thirdly, as mentioned above, many of those on advanced courses in public sector higher education, and particularly those on part-time courses, would be taking professional courses of different levels, and also sub-degree qualifications such as diploma and certificate courses.

What Table 1 does show clearly is the preponderance of older students on part-time courses — students aged 25 or over constituted about two-thirds of those on part-time courses as opposed to only 15.3 per cent of those on full-time courses. It is important to note, however, that the provision of part-time undergraduate courses at universities is very limited (apart, of course, from the Open University which provides degrees by distance study methods) and that the overwhelming majority of those on part-time courses are attending polytechnics and other public sector institutions of higher education. The data in Table 2 provides a more accurate indication of mature students in higher education by focusing on age at enrolment. It gives longitudinal information on mature new enrolments in universities (in the United Kingdom) and public sector colleges (in England and Wales) over the period 1978 to 1982. Whereas mature entrants represented 12 per cent of new undergraduates in universities in 1982, they represented almost one-third of all new entrants on degree courses in public sector colleges. However, the fact that the proportion of mature students on degree courses in public sector colleges has declined from a peak of 39 per cent in 1979 to just over 30 per cent in 1982 has caused some concern and the Continuing Education Working Party of the National Advisory Board, responsible for public sector higher education, has recommended that NAB plan for an increase in these numbers as one of the strategic objectives of its 1987/88 planning exercises.

Table 1
STUDENTS ON ADVANCED COURSES IN UNIVERSITIES, POLYTECHNICS AND OTHER PUBLIC SECTOR INSTITUTIONS, AND THE OPEN UNIVERSITY IN THE UNITED KINGDOM (1983/84) (1)

Mode of study	Total (000's)	Number (000's)	Proportion aged 25 or over 1
Full-time	580.5	88.7	15.3%
Part-time	313.2	195.8	62.5%
Total Number	893.7	284.5	31.8%

Source: Social Trends 16 (1986). Central Statistical Office.
1. Includes undergraduates, postgraduates, those on other advanced courses and 46 600 students from abroad. Figures for the Open University include associate students.

Table 2
MATURE NEW ENTRANTS AS A PROPORTION OF THE TOTAL NUMBER OF NEW ENTRANTS 1978—82 (1)

	1978	1979	1980	1981	1982
Public Sector Higher Education (2)					
First Degree and equivalent	36.2	38.9	35.3	32.6	30.5
Other advanced	60.6	62.1	59.9	59.6	57.9
Post-graduate	52.1	52.6	50.8	48.8	50.6
Universities (3)					
Under-graduates	13.4	12.9	12.8	13.1	12.0
Post-graduates	37.9	38.5	38.5	38.1	38.9

1. Mature entrants on degree level are those aged 21 or over; on post-graduate courses, those aged 25 or over on entry.
2. NAB Report, Appendix 5 (refers to England and Wales).
3. UGC Report, Appendix 4 (refers to the United Kingdom). Does not include the Open University.

Table 3 shows the sex distribution of students in higher education by age group. Generally, men were more likely to be students in higher education than women, and age had little impact on this distribution.

Table 3

SEX OF STUDENTS ON ADVANCED COURSES IN UNIVERSITIES, POLYTECHNICS AND OTHER PUBLIC SECTOR COLLEGES, THE OPEN UNIVERSITY, IN THE UNITED KINGDOM 1983/84

Mode of study	Male (000's)	Female (000's)	Proportion of female students
Full—Time			
Under 25	280-1	211-7	43%
25 and over	54-3	34-4	38.7%
Part—Time			
Under 25	89-4	28-0	23.8%
25 and over	120-5	75-3	38.4%
Total	544-3	349-4	39.1%

Source: Social Trends 16 (1986). Central Statistical Office.

The following paragraphs in this section broadly describe the higher education system in the United Kingdom. Practically all the issues covered here will be raised in more detail in subsequent sections, where particular reference will be made to the implications for mature students.

2. *Admission to First Degree Courses*

Applications for admission to first degree courses at universities in England and Wales (except for the Open University) are submitted through the Universities' Central Council on Admissions (UCCA). The candidate applies to up to five universities or colleges listed in order of preference, in the autumn term of the academic year preceding admission. UCCA copy this to each of the institutions named, who are responsible for selecting their own students. The same procedure usually applies in Scotland and Northern Ireland.

A similar centralised system for application to full-time courses in Polytechnics was introduced in 1986. Applications for entry to courses in art and design are made through the Art and Design Admissions Registry and, in education, through the Central Register and Clearing House. These institutions each co-ordinate applications and admissions to polytechnics and other institutions of higher education. Applications for entry to part-time degree courses at polytechnics are made direct to the individual polytechnic (on a common application form) or by various means to other institutions. Some colleges invite applications to their diversified courses only through the Central Register and Clearing House, some require applications to be made direct to the college; and some allow the candidate to choose which procedure to follow.

Each validating body is responsible for drawing up its own regulations about admission, and requirements for a particular type of course will vary in detail from body to body and therefore from institution to institution. All institutions in considering applications for entry to higher education courses will not only look for a satisfactory standard of general education (including an ability to speak and understand English well) but more specifically will require a minimum of five passes in the General Certificate of Education (GCE) or the

Scottish Certificate of Education (SCE), including two at advanced level (3). A grade 1 pass in the Certificate of Secondary Education (CSE) is reckoned as equivalent to a GCE at ordinary level. An International or European Baccalaureate may also be acceptable. Some universities will not admit students wishing to study for a degree in arts and science for any period shorter than the usual three or four years, though some will allow students with an overseas degree qualification to complete the course in two years. Mature students, normally aged 23 or over, may be acceptable without formal qualifications if they have suitable experience.

3. Structure of Degree Courses

In England, Wales and Northern Ireland, the best known first degrees are B.A. (Bachelor of Arts) and B.Sc. (Bachelor of Science) which offer a general qualification in a wide range of subject choices. Other degrees tend to be related to a profession, for example MB or ChB (Medicine), LLB (Law) and B.Ed. (Bachelor of Education), though some have a relevance wider than the profession to which they are directly related. Courses usually last three or four years though some, for example, Medicine and Dentistry, take longer. In Scotland, the first degree is a four-year degree (MA or B.Sc.) with honours, or a three-year broad-based ordinary degree, which is a particular feature of the Scottish system.

Courses normally require full-time or "sandwich" attendance (i.e. alternating periods of course work and practical training) and may cover one or more than one subject (joint or combined degrees). Course options and modular structures for degrees allow flexibility within course provision at particular institutions, and it is at the discretion of institutions and validating bodies to determine what subjects should be prescribed for a particular course of study.

4. Funding of Higher Education Institutions

The Government makes funds available to universities by way of recurrent grant, furniture and equipment grant, and capital building grant. These account for about 70 per cent of university income. A further 20 per cent is derived from fees charged to students: students in receipt of an award have these paid by the award making body (usually the local education authority). Income and expenditure from research contacts are intended to be broadly in balance.

Allocations of recurrent grant to individual universities follow advice from the University Grants Committee (UGC), which by convention is not questioned by the Secretary of State, and are normally made in the form of a block grant to each university. The Committee explains to each university the factors on which the grant has been based, but it is for the university to determine its internal distribution. Occasionally, the UGC may make earmarked grants to stimulate particular developments but these are usually incorporated into the block grant as soon as possible. Furniture and equipment grant is also made available to each university as a block grant; whilst capital grants are allocated for projects approved by the UGC on a project by project basis.

Expenditure on institutions maintained by local authorities attracts central government support, in common with other local authority activities, via the Rate Support Grant (RSG) and is otherwise funded from local authority rates. Because higher education institutions are reckoned to provide a national service, the cost of provision is shared or "pooled" among all authorities. A limit is now set to the total amount which may be pooled each year and this is apportioned among providing authorities by the Secretary of State on the advice of the National Advisory Body for Local Authority Higher Education. Each authority may, however, spend more than the amount allocated to it if it wishes, finding the extra finance entirely from its own rate fund.

5. *Voluntary-Aided and Direct Grant Colleges*

Grant-aided colleges are mainly voluntary denominational colleges of education, receiving a large part of their income in grant aid, and specialist institutions, for music for example, financed directly by central government. All colleges are open to students of all religious persuasions or none, in common with all other institutions of higher education.

6. *Financing Fees and Maintenance Costs*

The main source of financing for students comes through state mandatory and discretionary grants. Students who satisfy the conditions of the Education (Mandatory Awards) Regulations qualify for a maintenance grant and the payment of their fees. No mandatory financial support is available from central or local government funds for students undertaking part-time degree courses or distance studies. Discretionary grants are payable by local education authorities to students failing to satisfy the conditions for receipt of mandatory grant, including those students on part-time degree courses or distance studies. Such grants are at the rates and conditions set by the authorities. Financial support is available to students irrespective of age. Students of 25 years or over, however, are regarded as having independent status and do not have their maintenance grant abated by a parental contribution. Independent students can, according to their circumstances, qualify for small supplements to their grant and an additional maintenance grant is also available to students with family responsibilities.

B. CHARACTERISTICS OF MATURE STUDENTS IN HIGHER EDUCATION

This section presents a profile of mature students in higher education in England and Wales. Because most of the official statistics are limited in scope and are not very compatible with the definitions being employed for purposes

31

of this study, the findings of a recent survey of mature students throughout England and Wales will be drawn upon for supplementary data. The Mature Students Research Project was commissioned in 1980 by the Department of Education and Science with the objective of providing a comprehensive information on the characteristics, motivations, needs and problems of mature students in all forms of education (4). A "Mature Student" was defined for the purpose of the survey as being a student who was "undertaking a course of a substantial nature, provided by an educational body, in the academic year 1980-81, who was aged 21 or over on entry to the course".

The range of courses and institutions covered by the survey was extremely wide. Questionnaires were distributed to mature students undertaking qualifying courses (of all levels) at universities, the Open University, polytechnics and other public sector colleges of further and higher education, commercial correspondence colleges and long-term residential colleges. A further 5 000 were distributed to those on non-qualifying courses (see Chapter II for a discussion of this aspect of the survey).

The data from the Mature Students Project has been reworked specially for this report in an attempt to present the information in a form as close to that suggested as possible. The tables, therefore, refer to respondents aged 25 or over, although in some cases information for those aged 21 to 25 is presented for comparative purposes. The data is broken down into four institutional categories. Firstly, there are mature students undertaking first degrees at universities (5). Secondly, there are mature students undertaking first degrees at the Open University (6). The other two categories represent the public sector (7). Although in official parlance this definition includes polytechnics it was decided to present them separately because they represent the major public sector higher education institutions, and because in many cases it is interesting to compare them directly to the university sector.

1. Marital and Family Status
Table 4 shows the marital and family status of mature students in the survey. This is an important issue as it highlights the responsibilities of the mature students and is an indication of their other commitments and demands on their time, energy and finances:

The figures for the different types of institutions tend to reflect to some extent their different age profiles. Thus, about half of those at polytechnics and universities (51 per cent and 55 per cent respectively) are living with a spouse with or without children as opposed to approximately three-quarters of those attending other colleges or the Open University (72 per cent and 75 per cent respectively). The proportion of mature students living as single parents is similar across all institutions.

Table 4
LIVING SITUATION OF MATURE STUDENTS (25+) IN HIGHER EDUCATION IN ENGLAND AND WALES (SURVEY DATA, PERCENTAGES)

Living Situation	Polytechnics	Other Colleges	Universities	Open University
Spouse	29	22	26	15
Spouse and children	32	50	29	60
Children only		7	9	9
Alone or other	32	21	36	15

Source: Mature Students Research Project

2. *Educational Background*

Table 5 shows the highest educational qualification achieved by students on entry to their courses. Later sections will discuss in more detail alternative entry procedures (see Section C); it is however interesting to note here that although the Open University and polytechnics seem to be relatively more successful in attracting mature students into higher education with no qualifications whatsoever, the proportions falling into this category are, in fact, very small at 6 per cent and 3 per cent respectively. When we look at those with generally "low" qualifications, however, two groups of institutions emerge — on the one hand, there are the universities and polytechics with 9 per cent and 12 per cent respectively having no qualifications or qualifications below "A" level, while on the other hand, 24 per cent of those at other colleges and 26 per cent of those at the Open University are in this category. At the other end of the scale, almost half of those at all institutions had already achieved a high educational standard before embarking on their present higher education course.

Table 5
HIGHEST EDUCATIONAL QUALICATIONS ON ENTRY OF MATURE STUDENTS (25+) TO HIGHER EDUCATION (SURVEY DATA, PERCENTAGES)

Entry Qualifications	Polytechnics	Other Colleges	Universities	Open University
No formal qualifications	3	1	1	6
Below "A" level	9	23	8	20
"A" level or equivalent	43	32	43	23
Above "A" level	45	44	49	51

Source: Mature Students Research Project

It is interesting to compare the pattern across all institutions with that of the adult population at large. As Table 6 shows, mature students in higher education tend to have achieved a considerably higher level of education than most of the population. Whilst this must be interpreted with caution as the population figures include a lot of older people, it certainly poses questions of access to higher education. The figures for mature students aged 21 or over in both further and higher education courses in a wide range of institutions are also given for comparative purposes.

Table 6

COMPARISON OF EDUCATIONAL LEVEL OF MATURE STUDENTS IN HIGHER EDUCATION (SURVEY DATA) WITH THAT OF THE GENERAL ADULT POPULATION

	Mature Students in Higher Education Aged 25 or over(1)	Mature Students in Further and Higher Education Aged 21 or over(2)	Adult Populations (3)
	%	%	%
No qualifications	4	9	52
Below "A" level	20	30	23
"A" level or equivalent	31	28	5
Above "A" level	45	34	15
Foreign or other	—	—	4

1. Mature Student Research Project Weighted Total.
2. Mature Student Research Project — includes mature students aged 21 or over on courses of all levels at polytechnics, other colleges, universities, Open University, Residential Colleges, and correspondence colleges.
3. Office of Population Census and Surveys. General Household Survey, 1980, HMSO (covers Great Britain).

3. Employment Status

Table 7 shows that it is students at the Open University and polytechnics who are most likely to be in paid employment of some kind — with three-quarters of the former and 63 per cent of the latter falling into this category. Obviously all respondents by definition fit the category of "student" but they had the opportunity to select some other employment status if they felt this to be more significant. The highest proportion of those who described themselves as house-wives, was to be found at the Open University (15 per cent) which also had the highest proportion of retired people (4 per cent). Those who were unemployed constituted 3 per cent of those at polytechnics and the Open University, 2 per cent at other colleges and 1 per cent of those at universities.

Table 8 gives the occupational grouping of those adults who were in employment. There is not much difference between mature students at the different institutions; what is striking is that the majority in all colleges come from the professional and more senior service positions, and that people from other non-manual and manual positions were definitely under-represented when compared to the distribution of the population at large.

Table 7
EMPLOYMENT STATUS OF MATURE STUDENTS (25+)IN HIGHER EDUCATION IN ENGLAND AND WALES (SURVEY DATA, PERCENTAGES)

Employment Status	Polytechnics	Other Colleges	Universities	Open University
In Paid Employment (full-time or part-time):	63	41	26	75
Not in Paid Employment:				
Full-time housekeeper	2	5	2	15
Retired	0	0	1	4
Unemployed	3	2	1	3
Full-time student	30	50	68	1
Other (e.g. disabled)	2	1	1	1
Total not emplayed:	37	58	73	24

Source: Mature Students Research Project

Table 8
OCCUPATIONAL GROUPING OF MATURE STUDENTS (25+)IN HIGHER EDUCATION IN ENGLAND AND WALES (SURVEY DATA, PERCENTAGES)

Occupational Grouping	Polytechnics	Other Colleges	Universities	Open University
Professional and service	72	65	64	74
Other − non-manual	18	20	22	16
Manual	10	15	14	10

Source: Mature Students Research Project

Table 9 shows the types of organisations in which respondents from the different institutions were employed at the time. A number of interesting patterns emerge − for example, about a quarter of students at all institutions except public sector colleges other than polytechnics, worked in some form of public administration. Those involved in education also comprised a large proportion of higher education mature students ranging from 23 per cent at polytechnics to 38 per cent at the Open University, 26 per cent at universities and 67 per cent at other colleges. The Open University appeared to be the most successful in attracting students working in manufacturing, production and construction, while on the other hand polytechnics appeared relatively more successful in attracting those working in the health service and in sales and distribution.

Table 9

**TYPE OF ORGANISATION IN WHICH MATURE STUDENTS (25+) IN
HIGHER EDUCATION ARE CURRENTLY EMPLOYED (SURVEY DATA,
PERCENTAGES)**

Organisation	Polytechnics	Other Colleges	Universities	Open University
1. Insurance, Banking, Finance and Business	3	3	0	1
2. Manufacturing, Production, Construction	9	4	4	17
3. Sales and Distribution	9	3	5	2
4. Professional and Scientific	7	1	6	3
5. Miscellaneous Services	4	5	5	3
6. National Health Service	11	4	6	4
7. Nationalised Industries	5	8	5	7
8. Public Administration and Defence	28	6	24	25
9. Educational Services	23	67	46	38

Source: Mature Students Research Project

4. Field of Study

Table 10 shows the field of study of mature students in the Mature Student
Project Survey. These have been grouped into three broad headings — science,
social science and arts. Students at the Open University were more likely to be
studying in a scientific subject (45 per cent) than those at other colleges. Within
this general field of study, there were quite clear areas of specialisation —
polytechnics had the highest proportion of engineering students (22 per cent),
the Open University had the highest proportion of science students (33 per
cent) and universities had the highest proportion of medical students (16 per
cent). Social Science was studied by 36 per cent of those at universities, 25 per
cent of those at polytechnics, 22 per cent of those at the Open University and 7
per cent of those at other colleges. Polytechnics had the highest proportion of
mature students on professional and vocational courses (19 per cent) while they
had the lowest proportion in Arts based subjects (6 per cent). Other colleges of
further and higher education had the highest proportion of creative courses
(e.g. drama) while the Open University had the highest proportion in the Arts
(25 per cent).

Table 10
FIELD OF STUDY OF MATURE STUDENTS (25+)
IN HIGHER EDUCATION (SURVEY DATA, PERCENTAGES)

Field of Study	Polytechnics		Other Colleges		Universities		Open University	
Scientific Subjects								
Medical	3		0		16		0	
Engineering	22		5		2		12	
Agriculture	0		0		1		0	
Science	<u>10</u>	35	<u>11</u>	16	<u>8</u>	27	<u>33</u>	45
Social Sciences								
Education	5		27		3		2	
Social Science	25		7		36		22	
Professional and Vocational	19		1		3		0	
Business	<u>9</u>	58	<u>5</u>	40	<u>1</u>	43	<u>0</u>	24
Arts								
Languages	2		12		13		2	
Arts	2		11		15		25	
Creative	<u>2</u>	6	<u>20</u>	43	<u>1</u>	29	<u>4</u>	31

Source: Mature Students Research Project

For comparative purposes it is interesting to look at the fields of study undertaken by different age groups of students. Table 11 shows the areas of study of students entering universities in Great Britain in 1981 by age groups. It is quite clear that the older the entrant to a university is, the more likely she/he is to opt for the Social Sciences (which includes Business and Professional courses) while the younger they are the more likely to opt for science based subjects. The age differences were not so great for Arts subjects, although mature students appeared to be more inclined to opt for them than the younger students.

Table 11
FIELD OF STUDY OF HOME STUDENTS ACCEPTED FOR UNIVERSITY
ENTRANCE IN GREAT BRITAIN BY AGE GROUP (1981)

Field of Study	Percentages		
	Under 21	21 – 24	25 +
Science and related subjects	50	46	24
Social Sciences	27	33	42
Arts Subjects	23	21	33

Source: 1. UCCA. Statistical Supplement to 19th Report. Adapted from Table 82.

5. Mode of Study

Table 12 shows the mode of study of mature students in the survey. It is apparent that, apart from colleges of further and higher education, mature students are far more likely than younger students to be part-time students.

The striking difference is between those at universities and polytechnics. The latter were far more likely to be part-time students than those at universities and in fact the difference is likely to be greater as, for sampling reasons, the proportion of part-time students at universities in the survey is likely to be somewhat larger than in the population of university students.

Table 12
MODE OF STUDY OF MATURE STUDENTS (25+)
IN HIGHER EDUCATION (SURVEY DATA, PERCENTAGES)

	Other			*Open*
Mode of Study	Polytechnics	Colleges	Universities	University
	21−24 25+	21−24 25+	21−24 25+	21−24 25+
Full-time	58 40	56 57	97 86	0 0
Part-time	42 60	43 43	3 14	100 100

Source: Mature Students Research Project

C. POLICIES AND PRACTICE OF INSTITUTIONS OF HIGHER EDUCATION CONCERNING ADULT STUDENTS

1. Admissions

The general minimum entry requirements for degree level courses are five General Certificate of Education (GCE) passes, including two at Advanced level ("A" level). In Scotland the equivalent requirement is five Scottish Certificates of Education (SCE) passes including three at Higher Grade. These represent the most common entry routes to degree level courses but certain other qualifications are also accepted as normal — for example, Ordinary National Certificate/Diploma (ONC/D) at a good standard and certain City and Guilds Final Technicians Certificates. In recent years approximately 90 per cent of all full-time home undergraduates in universities entered with at least two "A" levels while about 80 per cent in the public sector on similar courses had these qualifications. In the public sector, however, entrants to higher level courses other than degrees were far less likely to have come through this route with this trend being even more pronounced for part-time courses (8).

Within this dominant framework there is, however, room for flexibility, particularly in the case of mature applicants. The Council for National Academic Awards (CNAA), for example, points out that:

"While the normal entry qualifications may be one of the best available indications of academic potential among school leavers, they are not necessarily an appropriate measure of the ability of mature students aged 21 or over" (9).

Most universities also allow room for discretion in the case of special groups of applicants such as mature students. Table 13 shows that applicants in the older age groups were far less likely to have entered university with "A" levels than younger students, and that this difference increased with age. On the other hand the older an entrant was, the more likely he/she was to have been admitted on the basis of unspecified "other U.K. qualifications" — over half of those who were 40 or over (53 per cent) came into this category as opposed to none of those under 21 and only 7 per cent of those aged 21 to 25. In spite of these trends, however, the fact remains that a clear majority of those in the 21 to 39 age group, who constitute the main bulk of mature students at universities, entered with "A" levels or the conventionally recognised alternatives.

Although, as has been pointed out, individual institutions have the discretion to accept mature students on whatever basis they choose to establish, several formal schemes have been instituted with the specific objective of providing more systematic methods of assessing mature student applicants. It is useful here to consider a few examples. One such scheme, called the Open College project, involves a number of colleges of further education, a polytechnic and a university in the particular geographic area of the North-West of England. Special course units are undertaken at any of the colleges of further education, and are assessed by course work rather than exams. The intention is to offer an adult alternative to GCE "A" levels, and the work is accepted as such by the institutions of higher education involved in the scheme.

Table 13
THE ENTRY QUALICATIONS OF A SAMPLE OF ACCEPTED UNIVERSITY CANDIDATES IN 1979

Qualifications	Under 21	21—25	26—39	40 and over
GCE "A" Levels	92.6	66.2	45.5	31.1
Scottish Qualifications	5.4	4.6	5.4	2.2
ONC/D	1.2	3.1	5.7	2.2
HNC/D	0.1	10.2	4.5	4.4
Degree	-	4.1	2.0	2.2
Other U.K. Qualifications	-	6.6	32.0	53.3
Overseas Qualifications	0.4	2.8	2.5	4.4
Unidentified Qualifications	0.3	2.5	2.5	—
TOTAL NUMBER	6 940.0	393.0	244.0	45.0

Source: 1. UCCA Statistical Supplement to the 17th Report.

Similar relationships between a local college of further education and higher education are emerging all the time, although, in general, polytechnics are more to the forefront in such schemes than the universities. These preparatory courses usually take the form of "Return to Study", "Access", "Fresh Horizons" or "New Opportunities for Women" courses. There appear to be two problems about such schemes from the student's point of view. Firstly, the links are often between a limited number of departments within the institution of higher education and thus do not open the way to all areas of study. Secondly, while the preparatory courses may be accepted by institutions other than the one with which it is directly linked, there is no guarantee of this should the student desire to go elsewhere.

An example of a scheme which has been in operation for many years is the Northern Universities Joint Matriculation Board Scheme for Mature Entry. Five universities are involved in the scheme which provides a special test "of a nature suitable for mature candidates who may have very different educational backgrounds". Other universities, for example, Sussex University, have established similar schemes of their own, which generally include an essay, an oral examination, a general paper and subject questions.

An important variation on the pattern described above is provided by Birkbeck College of London University. It may enrol an unqualified mature student provisionally for the first year. If the student is successful in the first year, he may then continue on the degree programme.

It is the Open University which has adopted the most radical approach to mature student admissions. No formal qualifications are required on entry and while quotas are applied based on regional regulations, courses of study and students' occupations, the method of accepting students is essentially "first come, first served". The Open University plays a further role in increasing access as Open University credits can be used as the basis for entering conventional higher education establishments. (This is considered in more detail when discussing credit transfers.)

While this brief review does indicate some willingness to accept "unconventional" entry qualifications as the basis for mature student entry to higher education, there remains the question of the chances of mature applicants who have no formal qualifications whatsoever. The Advisory Council for Adult and Continuing Education, for example, expresses some reservations about how innovatory some "unconventional" entry schemes actually are. It points to a fairly high failure rate in some schemes and comments that one scheme:

> "... has been criticised as a disincentive in that it requires preparation of a general kind (a mathematics paper is commonly required in practice) that disadvantages a student who has a clear subject interest in view and who has already been attending classes in it. In other words the test operates, like "A" levels, as a self-contained selection device rather than a preparation for further study" (10).

While there are no population figures available, the survey results referred to in Section B indicate that the proportion of mature students entering higher education with no formal qualifications whatsoever appears to be relatively low at about 4 per cent.

It is important to note that although the various higher education bodies, and most of the colleges themselves, make reference to the desirability of alternative entry routes for mature students, the way in which this general policy is translated into practice varies quite greatly between institutions. The percentage of mature undergraduate students in U.K. universities varied between a low of 2 per cent and a high of about 16 per cent in 1979 (11). Although in general the public sector institutions attract a higher proportion of mature students, institutional differences certainly remain.

2. Credit Transfer

While the flexibility inherent in the system of credit transfer is generally acknowledged as being of benefit to students, and to adult students in particular, it is only being gradually introduced on a small number of higher level courses in polytechnics and universities. Qualifications being provided on a modular basis by the Technician Education Council and Business Education Council represent examples of moves in this direction. The main exception to the rule is the Open University, where the whole degree structure is based on a credit system, and where Open University credits are recognised for purposes of transferring to conventional degree courses. The Advisory Council outlines some of the advantages it sees in a system of credit transfer:

> "Adults studying part-time can inevitably find their studies disrupted by the need to change jobs and move house. They need to be able to transfer in mid-stream to another course in another institution without losing academic standing; others may want to change into another subject area. Such transfers are undoubtedly easier, and sometimes only possible if courses are constructed on a modular basis" (12).

They do, however, recognise some of the main difficulties involved. For example, frequently:

> ". . . there is still no agreement about the equivalence of those modular courses and their levels. In particular there remains the difficult question of the validity of qualifications over time" (13).

Another problem was raised in an earlier report:

> "The difficulties arise with locally validated examinations such as a college diploma or a university degree. Each institution's course is separately devised and taught, so that entry midway through requires an individual assessment of how far the early ground of the course has been covered already" (14).

The other main problem identified was that of providing the comprehensive information system without which any developments would be bound to stay local.

As the Department of Education and Science has pointed out, an important way of catalysing the development of a flexible modular approach:

> ". . . is by ensuring that co-operation about credit transfer and advance standing is adequately disseminated to students, institutions and other interested parties. This would not only enable the full potential of existing arrangements to be achieved but would serve to encourage the further development and wider acceptance of modular courses and advance standing arrangements" (15).

Following the recognition by the Russell Report (16) that there was a growing need for a transferable credit structure the Department of Education and Science commissioned a feasibility study for a credit transfer information system. They sought the opinions of all those who would be involved in any such scheme — the award-making institutions, advisory services and the students themselves. There was general agreement that credit transfer information systems would be seen as providing an extremely useful service. The report concluded that it would be feasible to establish a national information service which would both record and provide information on credit transfer possibilities (17).

The report suggested it would take about five years before a comprehensive service could be offered. Recognising the importance of the whole area, the Department of Education and Science has recently established a pilot project under the title of Educational Counselling and Credit Transfer Information Service (ECCTIS).

> "Apart from the fact that much of the information in the Toyne Report was becoming out of date and the need to examine more closely the counselling aspects of ECCTIS, there remained a number of unresolved practical problems including effective means of collecting all the data required" (18).

It is hoped that a national system will be developed on the basis of the experience of the pilot project.

Another public sector scheme which was launched by the Department of Education and Science in 1982 is the Professional, Industrial and Commercial Updating Programme (PICKUP). This programme has the aim of stimulating the development of mid-career vocational courses. As well as providing information on post-experience vocational education opportunities in polytechnics and other institutions, this programme is designed to assist the development of flexible administrative and academic structures for this type of work.

In considering credit for life experience and experiential learning in 1982, the Advisory Council for Adult and Continuing Education commented:

> "The principle of open educational access for adults is implicitly, if not explicitly, based on the idea that the experience adults have gained in their lives and work can contribute to their studies" (19).

They pointed out that the pressure being exerted in other countries for credit to be given for life experience, as distinct from the conventionally accepted methods of organised learning, had not yet really occurred in Britain. Even the Open University, although it has open access, only gives credit for prior educational experience at the higher education level. However, an initiative launched early in 1986 indicates developments in this area. The Council for National Academic Awards (CNAA) — the validating body for public sector higher education — launched a Credit Accumulation and Transfer Scheme (CATS) designed to ease movement between institutions, and to give credit for work and other life experience.

3. Attendance Options

First degree programmes are readily available as full-time courses in universities, polytechnics and a number of other institutions. They are available by correspondence study through the Open University, which is, as has been described already, an institution particularly geared towards the needs of adults. In relation to part-time study in universities, a recent study commented:

> "The provision of part-time undergraduate study opportunities in the conventional universities is extremely limited. The only university institution in the whole of the United Kingdom which is fully geared to the provision of part-time face-to-face teaching at this level is Birkbeck College, part of the University of London. In all, only eleven out of the 44 conventional universities currently make some formal part-time undergraduate provision in subjects other than education" (20).

The situation is generally better in polytechnics where more provision is made for part-time degrees — all of the polytechnics in England and Wales offer at least one part-time degree, and one offered eighteen part-time degrees in 1980-81 (21).

Apart from Birkbeck, which was developed specially for the purpose, there are three main types of undergraduate part-time provision. Firstly, in the universities part-time degrees may be organised through an extra-mural department, although staff from other departments may do most or all of the teaching on any one course (22). Secondly, both universities and polytechnics may offer specially designed part-time degrees — usually in the evening. Finally, some colleges have opened up their conventional undergraduate courses to part-time students where they study alongside full-time students. Part-time degrees last, on average, five years for an Honours Degree. Although figures are not readily available, it is likely that the vast majority of students on these courses are mature students.

4. Information and Counselling Services for Adults

Most institutions do, of course, issue a brochure or prospectus giving full details of their courses and may advertise in local libraries, the local press, and, to a lesser extent, local radio and television. Informal advice and counselling is generally available from a range of staff members, and some institutions have a post with special responsibility for counselling and contributing to the general welfare of mature students.

The Advisory Council on Adult and Continuing Education published in 1979 a study of the growing number of local schemes, providing information and counselling services for adults. It pointed out that at the moment adults could seek information from a "bewildering" variety of possible sources — libraries, citizens' advice bureaux, job centres, local newspapers and local radio as well as the institutions themselves. However, there is little attempt to co-ordinate these, and they concluded that:

"These local guidance services should be co-operative and collaborative ventures, rather than the exclusive preserve of any one professional group or institution" (23).

In 1981, a Directory of Educational Guidance Services for Adults was published listing 40 such ventures throughout the country — this had increased from a total of 18 in 1979 (24).

These local services certainly represent attempts to meet the educational information and advisory needs of adults. It was recommended that various strategies should be adopted which could be viewed as pilot projects. For example, three possible organisational arrangements were identified:

a) The "Link Chain" type where a directory of volunteers is maintained and an individual potential student can contact the most appropriate volunteer;
b) The "Centre" type which offers a centralised service, often with professional trained staff; and
c) The "Link Chain Centre" type which attempts to combine the positive features of both types.

An example of one pilot-scheme in this area has been mentioned above — the Educational Counselling and Credit Transfer Information Service (ECCTIS). One of the problems it is attempting to deal with is to devise a scheme for the computerisation of all data for ease of retrieval and updating.

The issue of guidance and counselling has been taken up as a priority by the recently founded Unit for the Development of Adult Continuing Education (UDACE). In 1985, it published a consultative document on "Helping Adults to Learn", which is an attempt to work towards a national policy on adult guidance.

While it is encouraging to note the interest and commitment being made to such schemes, the fact is that they are underfunded and so tend to be accessible only to a minority of adult students. Tables 14 and 15 rank the main sources of information and advice used by respondents in the Mature Students Research Project.

Table 14 shows mature students' perceptions of what they found to be the most useful source of information when taking up a higher education course. While there was a general agreement that a college prospectus, the staff at the college they were going to attend and a student who had taken the course previously were the main sources of information, some interesting differences emerged between mature students at the different institutions. Those at the Open University and conventional universities placed more emphasis on the value of a prospectus (60 per cent and 47 per cent respectively) compared to those at polytechnics and other colleges (33 per cent and 31 per cent respectively). Students at these latter colleges, on the other hand, were more likely to have found college staff or someone who had taken the course previously to be the most useful source of information than those at the Open University or conventional universities. Students at the Open University stand out as being the only ones to give any significant mention of radio and television sources of

44

information (6 per cent). Of interest for our purposes is the place awarded to specialist adult advisory services — they were cited as the most useful source of information by 4 per cent of mature students at polytechnics, 3 per cent of those at other colleges and 2 per cent of those at universities. Again, students at the Open University were unique in that not a single one over 25 mentioned these specialised services. Considering that these findings were based on students attending during 1980-81, and, as has been pointed out, specialised adult advisory services were only starting to expand in this period, they would certainly seem to have a potentially important role in providing information for adults interested in returning to study.

Table 14
RANK ORDERING OF MATURE STUDENTS' (25+) PERCEPTIONS OF THE MOST USEFUL SOURCE OF INFORMATION RECEIVED (SURVEY DATA)

	Polytechnics	%		*Other Colleges*	%
1.	Prospectus	33	1.	Prospectus	31
2.	College Staff (Present college)	21	2.	College Staff (Present college)	25
3.	Previous Student	17	3.	Previous Student	17
4.	College Staff (Previous college)	7	4.	Friend	7
5.	Work Colleague	6	5.	Spouse	4
			6.	Work Colleague	4
6.	Spouse	4	7.	College staff (Previous college)	3
7.	Friend	4			
8.	Specialised Adult Advisory Service	4	8.	Specialised Adult Advisory Service	3
9.	None or other	4	9.	None or other	4
	Universities	%		*Open University*	%
1.	Prospectus	47	1.	Prospectus	60
2.	College staff	13	2.	Previous student	15
3.	(Present college) Previous student	13	3.	Radio/television	6
4.	Friend	7	4.	Friend	3
5.	College staff (Previous college)	7	5.	College staff (Present college)	3
6.	Spouse	3	6.	Work colleague	3
7.	Work colleague	2	7.	Spouse	2
8.	Specialised Adult Advisory Service	2	8.	College staff (Previous college)	2
9.	None or other	6	9.	None or other	6

Source: Mature Students Research Project

Table 15 looks at the main sources of advice used by mature students in higher education. College staff, who were also listed as important sources of information again appear high on the list — being mentioned by 28 per cent of public sector college students, 19 per cent of polytechnic students and 17 per cent of university students. Only nine per cent of the Open University students (presumably because of its correspondence structure) mention receiving advice from staff members, although they still ranked staff in quite a high place. The polytechnic students stood out as unique in that a quarter of them found a work colleague the most useful source of advice, while only about six per cent to nine per cent of those at the other institutions of higher education saw them as being the most important source of advice. Specialist adult advisory services again occupy a small but fairly consistent position, as being the most useful source of advice.

Table 15
RANK ORDERING OF MATURE STUDENTS' (25+) PERCEPTIONS OF THE MOST USEFUL SOURCE OF ADVICE RECEIVED (SURVEY DATA)

	Polytechnics	%		*Other Colleges*	%
1.	Work colleagues	25	1.	College staff (present college)	28
2.	College staff (present college)	19	2.	Previous student	24
3.	Friend	12	3.	Friend	12
4.	Previous student	11	4.	Work colleague	9
5.	Prospectus	9	5.	Spouse	6
6.	Spouse	8	6.	College staff (previous college)	6
7.	College staff (previous college)	6	7.	Prospectus	5
8.	Specialised Adult Advisory Service	3	8.	Specialised Adult Advisory Service	4
	Others or none	7	9.	Others or none	6
	Universities	%		*Open University*	%
1.	College staff (present college)	17	1.	Previous student	28
2.	Friend	15	2.	Prospectus	21
3.	Previous student	13	3.	Spouse	10
4.	College staff (previous college)	12	4.	College staff (present institution)	9
5.	Spouse	12	5.	College staff (previous institution)	7
6.	Work colleague	9	6.	Friend	7
7.	Prospectus	5	7.	Work colleague	6
8.	Specialised Adult Advisory Service	5	8.	Specialised Adult Advisory Service	2
9.	Others or none	12	9.	Others or none	10

Source: Mature Students Research Project

D. MODES OF FINANCING FOR MATURE AGE STUDENTS

As has been pointed out, Local Education Authorities in England and Wales are generally responsible for making awards to students resident in their areas, and these awards can be divided into two types:

1. *Mandatory Awards*: Subject to certain conditions on residence, etc., in the United Kingdom LEAs have a duty to give awards to students following "designated" courses — these cover all first degree courses and comparable courses, including teacher training, Diploma in Higher Education, Higher National Diploma and Technician Education Council and Business Education Council Higher National Diploma Courses;

2. *Full Value Discretionary Awards*: Local Education Authorities may give awards at their discretion to students' who do not satisfy the residence, etc. conditions, but who are on "designated" courses; they may also give awards to students following other courses.

Mature students are eligible for two additional allowances — one is for the maintenance of dependents (spouse or other adult and/or children), the other is an older students' allowance (based on age).

Mandatory grants are paid by local education authorities which receive 90 per cent reimbursement from central government funds. Discretionary grants paid by local education authorities do not receive specific reimbursement. Central government funds are raised essentially through general taxes; local authority funds are raised through the rating system and are supplemented by a grant from central sources. Instances of an employer sponsoring a student on a first degree course are rare. But it may be possible for a student to receive limited financial assistance from industrial organisations or an educational charity or trust fund.

Tuition fees are normally paid direct to the educational establishment by the local education authority. Maintenance grant is paid direct to students, usually termly, and is normally obtainable through the academic office of the educational establishment.

In 1980/81, 379 407 students received full-value awards in England and Wales for further and higher education. Of these, 46 874 were "independent" students. An independent student is defined by the awards regulations as either "having attained the age of 25 years before the beginning of the year for which payments in pursuance of his award fall to be made, or has supported himself out of his earnings for periods before the first year of his course — aggregating not less than three years." Twenty-eight per cent of these award holders were attending a university, while the majority were at colleges of further and higher education. Forty-five per cent of these independent grant holders were female students, and one-third married. Unfortunately, it is not known exactly what courses these students were attending but the vast majority would be on degree level courses or equivalent.

Mature students are also eligible for an additional allowance for the maintenance of dependents (6 919 mandatory award holders received this allowance in 1980/81) and an older students grant (13 851 received this allowance in 1980/81). In addition to these main provisions every year a small number of Adult Education State Bursaries are awarded — these numbered 481 in 1980/81. These are awarded to mature students who are attending the one or two-year full-time courses at long-term adult residential colleges.

In an attempt to discover mature students' own views of their relative financial situation having returned to study, it is interesting to examine the information in Tables 16 and 17. This is based on the results of the Mature Students Research Project where respondents were asked about the impact of returning to study. Table 16 shows the percentage of respondents who mentioned certain costs of returning to study either in financial terms or benefits foregone.

It is obvious that there is a definite relationship between mode of study and costs in terms of employment, with those who are all studying part-time (the Open University) being the least likely to have to give up their work to take up study. It is notable that over one-third (38 per cent) of those at Universities and about one-fifth of those at polytechnics and other colleges had given up a full-time job to return to study. The fact that two per cent of those at universities and nine per cent of those at polytechnics felt they were giving up promotion opportunities certainly points to the importance of some form of paid educational leave being desirable at degree level.

Table 17 shows respondents' perceptions of their overall financial situation having returned to study. Here the part-time students seem to have lost their advantage, probably due to the fact that most will have paid their own fees.

Table 16
PERCENTAGE OF MATURE STUDENTS (25+) WHO MENTIONED CERTAIN COSTS OF RETURNING TO STUDY (SURVEY DATA PERCENTAGES)

	Polytechnic	Other Colleges	Universities	Open University
Loss of income through giving up full-time work	19	20	38	1
Loss of overtime earnings	10	9	10	4
Loss through giving up or reducing part-time work	13	16	17	8
Loss of promotion opportunities	9	15	25	1
Cost of child care	3	15	10	7
Other	4	10	13	7

Source: Mature Students Research Project

48

The proportion who said they were worse off for returning to education ranged from 32 per cent at polytechnics to 66 per cent at universities.

In relation to this problem of part-time students, the Advisory Council on Adult and Continuing Education offers as a suggestion that:

">. . . part-time students might be given an equivalent incentive in the form of income tax relief on the additional expenditure incurred in undertaking their studies and any relevant maintenance costs" (25).

Table 17
OVERALL FINANCIAL IMPACT OF RETURNING TO STUDY
FOR MATURE STUDENTS (SURVEY DATA PERCENTAGES)

Financial Situation	Polytechnic	Other Colleges	Universities	Open University
Worse off	32	44	66	50
About the same	57	44	25	46
Better off	10	13	9	4

Source: Mature Students Research Project

E. EVALUATION OF ADULT PARTICIPATION IN FULL (FIRST) DEGREE PROGRAMMES

1. Attitudes of Policy Makers

Increased mature student entry to higher education has been pointed to as one policy option against the background of an impending fall in the 18-year-old intake. Thus,

">. . . the demand which is already beginning to make itself felt, to devote more education resources to those already in employment might result in more systematic opportunities for recurrent education for mature students. Priority might be given at first to those who had missed higher education opportunities at normal entry age. But this might not preclude more radical developments, such as a systematic scheme for continuing education at an advanced level, or indeed at a non-advanced level" (26).

As has already been pointed out, the various bodies involved in higher education have highlighted the desirability of increasing mature student participation in higher education. The recent report on continuing education in the universities and public sector institutions places particular emphasis on attempting to reduce barriers to access for adult students.

The Advisory Council on Adult and Continuing Education sees its role as prompting wide debate on the ways in which our education service may move towards a more satisfactory system of continuing education. In contribution to this general purpose it published a report, Adult Students and Higher Education, which set out to establish some policy goals in the expansion of past-secondary education for adults and ways in which such expansion might be achieved.

Over the period 1981-82 a series of research-based seminars set out to undertake a major review of higher education in Britain and the reports of these Leverhulme seminars were then published in a series of papers. The issue of mature student participation was obviously one of the topics of interest. For example, one of the reports included a recommendation that at least 25 per cent of all admissions to higher education should be admitted with qualifications other than the conventional ones, and that:

> "... it should be the policy of government and of higher education institutions to encourage the participation of adults in courses of further and higher education at all levels, and to make appropriate provision for their special needs" (27).

2. Attitudes of Institutions

Turning to look at institutional policy, there are pragmatic reasons behind increased interest in mature students:

> "Left to themselves, institutions would have every reason to attract more students in the 1980s. The polytechnics and colleges already have a tradition of mixed age entry, but the impending shortfall of 18-year-olds has also concentrated the minds of the universities wonderfully in this direction. ... Instinctively, perhaps, higher education institutions see student demand as a defence — perhaps their only defence — against cuts. It is likely, therefore, that whatever policy is imposed upon them, they will try to attract as many applicants as possible. ... For many institutions, mature students could be seen as, at the least, an insurance policy, and, ideally, a relief column arriving at the siege" (28).

While there is some evidence to suggest that institutions and certain departments within institutions have certain fears about the abilities and possible special needs of the adult returning to study, in general they are gaining increasing recognition as something other than a marginal client group. Certainly in the last few years there has been a dramatic increase in the number of special access courses leading adults into higher education, and evidence of interest at an intitutional level in greater flexibility of modes of attendance.

3. Attitudes of Employers

This represents an area on which little research has been done to date. An investigation into paid educational leave (PEL) in the U.K. came to the following conclusions:

> "If the evidence of our survey is to be taken to indicate the preferences of employing organisations (first training for week excluded) then it appears that:
>
> a) In general they favour the making of in-house provision;
> b) In general, they favour very short courses, usually no more than six days for vocational training, and less than two days for Health and Safety training;
> c) Higher per capita rates are given for the purposes of management and supervision than for the training of other categories of the work;
> d) It is not clear that in-house PEL is given in any but marginal degrees towards purposes other than vocational training (which for managers and supervisors includes legal and industrial relations training), health and safety training and industrial relations training.

It is not known to what extent in-house vocational training includes liberal, remedial and other components" (29).

As will be seen in Chapter II, PEL is generally given for short periods of work-related study, it is unlikely therefore that employers are very enthusiastic about assisting adults to return to the far longer courses entailed in higher education studies.

In a study on employers' attitudes to Open University graduates, there is however some evidence of a more positive attitude to mature graduates even if employers do not wish to actually sponsor their studies:

> "Employers were clear that O.U. graduates differed in significant ways from ordinary graduates and usually viewed these as positive differences. Graduates were seen as "mature" rather than "old" and with a variety of positive personal characteristics; they were dedicated, serious, determined, more settled in their approach and more self-motivated" (30).

If thinking of offering any support for mature students, the study concluded that employers were mainly concerned about the extent to which it related to the employee's work or the firm's business.

4. *Effects of Undertaking Degree Studies on Later Economic Position*

Probably one of the other main gaps in research on mature students in Britain is in the area of the effects which participation has on their subsequent career prospects. While data is available on the first job graduates obtain on completing their course, unfortunately this is not broken down by age group.

One of the few studies undertaken on this topic was a follow-up study of Open University graduates undertaken in 1977. As this is of some considerable interest a fairly full summary is given below (31). At the time of the survey 43 per cent of the sample had only been graduates for 18 months or less.

> "Overall, one in two reported a good effect on their job or career, and as many as 18 per cent said they had experienced a marked good effect. In comparison, 18 per cent said their studies had had a mixed effect and two per cent a bad effect.
>
> Improving promotion prospects was the most widely reported benefit. Fifty per cent of teachers and 37 per cent of those in other occupations said they had already benefitted, and yet others expected to do so in the future (21 per cent and 17 per cent, respectively).
>
> A surprising proportion reported having 'developed a new career'. Often, of course, this is change within an occupational field or to a related field rather than a dramatic change to a totally unrelated job. One in three of housewives and one in five of non-teachers said they had made this kind of change as a consequence of their Open University studies and qualifications, and a further one in eight expected this outcome in the longer term. Of those reporting a very definite change, the following groups stood out: Forces (23 per cent), trades/transport (20 per cent), sales/services (20 per cent) and housewives (19 per cent). Over half the members of these groups had either made some kind of change or expected to do so. Fewer graduates in clerical/office and technical occupations reported change but over 40 per cent in each group expected to have developed a new career when the full effects of their studies and qualifications had been realised. Over two-thirds of

51

administrators/managers, qualified scientists and those in the professions and arts, were completely uninterested in a new career on entry and another 18 per cent or so thought it not very important. Even so, almost one in five had already made some change and half as many again expected to do so.

'It has meant that I have started to find myself as a person and has opened up the world' — a graduate.

Taking a very stringent criterion of benefit, the survey shows that the Open University qualifications had helped over a third of the sample (which comprised ten per cent of teachers graduating by December 1975 and 100 per cent of others) get a new job or post that was a substantial promotion or different in type from their previous jobs."

While this picture looks fairly optimistic for the mature graduate, another commentator points out that there are reasons for thinking that "older" mature students (over 30) may have greater difficulties in finding work — citing the upper age limits which, explicitly or implicitly, still exist in many areas of employment, and the stigma of "instability" which may attach to them if they have thrown up a previous job to study. However, as he points out it is difficult to assess the impact of vocational trends and therefore:

"... the individual adult is likely above all to perceive uncertainty: uncertainty created by technological, economic and political change. In those circumstances, the natural reaction perhaps is to hedge one's bets, and to see higher education not as an alternative, but as a complement to employment" (32).

Chapter II
Continuing education

A. BACKGROUND TO CONTINUING EDUCATION

1. Introduction

In 1975 the British Government accepted the principle of "éducation permanente" at the European Ministers of Education Conference at Stockholm.
There is, however, little agreement about where the boundaries, if any, should
be drawn with the types of activities traditionally encompassed within the term
"adult education". This debate has been going on for some time — thus, when
the Russell Committee on Adult Education was set up in 1969 its terms of
reference were to review "non-vocational" adult education. In the event,
however, the Committee rejected this concept as too narrow and instead
presented a view of a "comprehensive and flexible service of adult education,
broad enough to meet the whole range of educational needs of the adult in our
society" (33).

In 1977, the Advisory Council on Adult and Continuing Education was
established by the Secretary of State for Education with the following terms of
reference:

> To advise generally on matters relevant to the provision of education for adults in
> England and Wales and in particular:
> a) to promote co-operation between the various bodies in adult education and
>   review current practice, organisation and priorities, with a view to the most
>   effective deployment of available resources; and
> b) to promote the development of future policies and priorities, with full regard to
>   the concept of education as a process continuing throughout life.

In the Council's Report "Towards Continuing Education" they emphasize
this shift towards a broader definition by rejecting the vocational/non-voca-
tional division and suggesting that educational policy should simply distinguish between (a) "initial education", which covers schooling and any further or
higher education or training which directly follows-on from school; and
(b) "post-initial education", which covers all educational activities undertaken
by adults after a break from their initial education (34). This view of continuing

education is reflected in the DES discussion paper on "Continuing Education: Post Experience Vocational Provision for Those in Employment" which states:

> "Initial education can be defined as the continuous preparatory period of formal study, to whatever level, completed before entering main employment. Continuing education covers anything which follows" (35).

One of the practical problems ensuing from this broad definition of continuing education is the enormous difficulty of obtaining statistics on such diverse activities. Continuing education as it exists is not a "system"; it is rather a whole range of very disparate forms of provision. In this section, therefore, all we can hope to do is describe some of the main sources of continuing education for adults, point to the general type of programmes they provide, and briefly outline their organisational structure.

2. Local Education Authority Provision

Local Education Authorities (LEAs) constitute the main sources of continuing education through their adult education centres and colleges of further and higher education. These latter institutions provide both advanced or higher level courses (as discussed in Chapter 1) and non-advanced courses which are included in Table 18 (also includes courses not leading to any qualifications). In 1979 colleges of further and higher education had 980 000 students aged 21 or over enrolled on courses of all levels, which constituted 51 per cent of all enrolments. While quite a proportion of these would not strictly speaking be mature students (for example, some will be continuing courses started previously) it does give some indication of the patterns involved.

Table 18
MODE OF STUDY OF STUDENTS AT COLLEGES OF FURTHER AND HIGHER EDUCATION ON COURSES OF ALL LEVELS (1979)

Mode of Study	Under 21 (Percentage)	21 and Over (Percentage)
Full-time	35	17
Part-time day release	44	17
Other part-time day	3	14
Evening only	18	52
Total numbers	940 000	980 000
Students aged 21 and over as percentage of total:	–	51 %

Source: Adapted from Table 3, DES Statistical Bulletin 8/80.

LEAs also are responsible for what is the single largest source of education for adults through their local Adult Education Centres. These centres provide the forms of non-qualifying educational activities traditionally covered by the term "adult education". There are over 7 000 such centres throughout England and Wales — ranging from multi-purpose built centres providing a wide programme of courses during the day, evenings and weekends, to the use of school

54

premises during the evenings and term times only.

Although much of the work can be described as leisure-oriented, in fact local authority adult education has been at the forefront of many new developments. In a review of some of the most significant areas where LEA adult education have made the main input, ACACE highlighted the following (36):

a) Literacy and basic skills;
b) Programmes for immigrants and ethnic minorities;
c) Increased work with the mentally and physically handicapped; and
d) Work with disadvantaged parents with young children.

In 1979 there were about one and a half million students aged 18 or over attending courses in adult education centres, which constituted over 90 per cent of all enrolments. About 80 000 of these students would be attending literacy and basic education classes. All of these students are part-time and most of the students attending adult education centres do so in the evening, but there seems to be a trend towards more daytime participation. (In 1979 about 18 per cent were attending during the day.)

3. Universities and Responsible Bodies
Adult education has also been traditionally provided by the so-called "Responsible Bodies", which are designated "special responsible bodies for the provision of education for adults". The main such bodies are the extra-mural departments of universities, the Workers Educational Association (WEA) and the Welsh National Council of Young Men's Christian Associations. The extra-mural departments and the WEA provide many courses jointly and much of their work generally overlaps. In 1979-80, the extra-mural departments had over 161 000 students, the WEA over 117 000 and the Welsh National YMCA just over 1 000. The work of the university extra-mural departments will be considered in more detail in Section C of this Chapter, as will the continuing education work of the intra-mural university departments which particularly work in the area of professional updating.

4. Residential Colleges
There are seven long-term residential colleges which can cater for about 500 adult students. Although their number is small, these often provide very important links with universities and their courses often act as "gateways" to higher education. Some have particular links with the trade union movement and provide courses related to Industrial Relations. Most colleges provide bursaries and schemes of sponsorship.

5. Open University
Along with their undergraduate courses discussed in detail in Chapter 1, the Open University offers a continuing education programme which is designed primarily for adults who have had practical experience in a given field and who wish to develop or broaden their skills and understanding to a high level.

55

Again, this work will be considered in more detail in Section C of this Chapter. In 1980 there were about 8 000 associate students registered with the Open University.

6. *Manpower Services Commission*

The Manpower Services Commission was set up in 1974 under the Employment and Training Act of 1973 to run the public employment and training services. The New Training Initiative encompasses the first three of the Commission's objectives which are, firstly, to achieve the modernisation of occupational training, including apprenticeships; secondly, to prepare young people for work; and thirdly, to increase opportunities for adults (employed, unemployed, or returning to work) to acquire, increase or update their skills and knowledge during the course of their working lives.

Following the publication of a consultative document in 1983 on the development of an adult training strategy, there has been some shift in emphasis in relation to the training of adults. This is away from what is described as "speculative" training, and towards a focus on training and retraining for those in employment or about to start a new job. The argument is that this is the best way of achieving economic recovery.

The MSC has sponsored a number of major pump-priming projects based partially in institutions of further and higher education. One of these is the Open Tech, which is a programme designed to develop and deliver open learning programmes for technicians and supervisory level employees (37).

Another initiative has been sponsored jointly with the Department of Education and Science. These are Local Collaborative Projects, which are designed to encourage employers and course providers to work together in identifying training needs (particularly in the new technologies) and then organising appropriate activities to meet those needs. It is intended that employers would pay institutions of higher education the full cost for these programmes.

7. *Broadcasting*

It is extremely difficult to measure the contribution of radio and television to continuing education. The Open University will be considered separately, but it is important to note that all O.U. radio and television programmes can be received by the public at large as they are broadcast by the B.B.C. (British Broadcasting Corporation). The B.B.C. itself estimates that audiences for its own continuing education programmes on television vary from over 2 million for popular courses to about 50 000 on more specialist courses such as languages. Sales of learning materials associated with these programmes vary between 200 000 for a cookery course to 10 000 for a basic maths course. In the early 1980s the Independent Broadcasting Authority (I.B.A.) opened a new television station, Channel 4, which is financed from advertising revenue but which has an explicit brief to develop cultural and educational material. While formal evaluation of its success in meeting its objectives is very difficult, the station does appear to have made a significant contribution to the range and quality of educational material available to the community.

8. Other Sources of Continuing Education

There are a myriad of other organisations involved in the continuing education of adults which are impossible to document here — for example, there are the Trade Union Congress, individual unions, the armed forces and many professional bodies; there are also public authorities such as the Arts Council and the Sports Council, the libraries, the Health Education Council. Furthermore, there is a vast range of national and local voluntary and community groups who have an education role — for example, the National Federation of Townswomen's Guilds and the Co-operative Union.

9. Employers Involvement in Continuing Education

Britain is a signatory to the International Labour Office Convention (140) concerning Paid Education Leave (PEL), which states that in order to promote PEL each member country should:

> "... formulate and apply a policy designed to promote, by methods appropriate to national conditions and practice and by stages if necessary",

and that this should be achieved through collective bargaining.

PEL is regarded by the Advisory Council on Adult and Continuing Education as an important measure which would increase the availability to adults of existing educational provision. They point out that the bulk of that currently in existence has remained concerned with the training of young people, is concentrated in a small number of industries and has been extended very little to include even young women. In making a distinction between "education" and "job training", the Council raises the difficult issue of what activities should actually be included within the definition of PEL. Coupled with this definitional problem, the fact that much of the provision takes place on employers' premises makes it very difficult, if not impossible, to obtain comprehensive statistics relating to this aspect of education.

The Department of Education and Science recently sponsored a study which was to attempt to estimate the amount of PEL occurring in a particular year (38). Although the work relates to 1976-77 there have been no radical changes since then, and the work provides the most comprehensive overview of PEL in England and Wales. Much of the discussion in this section will therefore draw on this report. The "Education and Work" document defines the type of activities it includes as follows:

> "For the purposes of our survey, anything which satisfies the following conditions is Paid Educational Leave. Where a person who is an adult, working, employee, is given leave from his or her task to undertake any form of education or training being provided by any agency -- including the employee himself, where, during this period, the person in question is paid, by his employer, either his or her normal wage, or a sum of money calculated upon the basis of normal or average earnings

and intended to represent normal or average earnings (work related remuneration), although some loss of fringe benefits, special payments, compensations or overtime payments may result" (39).

It is important to note for present purposes that the Report defines as adult anyone over the age of 19 years.

The estimates of PEL in the study were based on five main sources of information:

1. A survey of further and higher educational institutions in 23 local education authorities;
2. A study of PEL in three professions -- law, medicine and related professions, and the church;
3. The courses provided in Teacher's Centres;
4. Private providers of courses for managers and related occupations;
5. A study of employers to estimate the amount of "in-house" PEL.

The approach adopted in the study was to undertake a survey in each of these areas, adjust the figures obtained for non-response and then gross up the figures to provide a population estimate. In doing this the authors emphasize that the figures must be taken as estimates due to the fact that it was impossible to actually undertake a random sample in this area and the figures are built from a variety of sources and from certain assumptions (40). The estimates exclude those on professional and degree courses, but:

> "... although considerable quantities of PEL (particularly measured in student days) are discernible among the excluded categories of provision, when compared with our national estimates of the number of student places for people in receipt of PEL and of the number of courses of study attended, they lead to virtually negligible increments (41).

They estimate, therefore, that the number of students over 19 receiving PEL during a year in the areas outlined here is in the region of one million.

Turning to consider PEL provided by employers, it is important to note that the study excluded informal on-the-job training from its definition of PEL (it also excluded small establishments employing less than 50 people from its survey). The study generally supports the view that the larger the establishment the more likely an employee is to enjoy "in-house" PEL. When in-house PEL is added to that provided in other institutions, the Education and Work study estimate that between three and four million people received some sort of PEL in 1976/77, which represents about one in six of all employed persons aged 19 or over.

An important problem to be highlighted by the report was the predominance of male students over female. For example, while two in five of all workers are female, only one in six of those who received PEL in a college is a woman. Patterns of segregation emerged − thus, while only 43 courses at colleges contained no men, 528 courses contained no women. In addition, men tended to predominate on those courses which were mixed. Two-thirds of the study of management centres and similar providers reported that at least 90 per cent of

PEL students were men.

For the purposes of this study on mature students in higher education it must be pointed out however that the vast bulk of the educational/training activities included in the Education and Work study would not fit within the definitions which we are applying. There are three main areas of difference. Firstly, they defined as an adult student anyone over the age of 19. Secondly, most of the courses were of very short duration, measured in days rather than years. Thirdly, little of the provision covered could be defined as higher education. Each of these points will be explored in an attempt to see how much of the PEL activities would seem to fall within our parameters.

The Education and Work report provides an estimate of the age distribution of PEL students in a whole range of educational institutions. As Table 19 shows, about two-thirds of the students were aged 25 or over. However, as the majority of students were aged 30 or under, it certainly appears that PEL is more likely to be obtained by younger adults. In summary, the report comments:

> "We have no direct indication of the age distribution for in-house provision, and we therefore confine our remarks to those courses run outside the employing organisation. Every pointer available to us indicates that PEL is so organised that its distribution by age groups runs directly contrary to the ideas of those who would see it as an essential part of any scheme for widespread continuing education. Not only is it more frequent among younger adults, but it is given for longer courses" (42).

Table 19
ESTIMATED PROPORTIONS OF PEL STUDENTS BY AGE GROUP
(SURVEY DATA)

Age Group	Percentage
19 — 24	33 %
25 — 30	25 %
31 — 50	33 %
50 +	9 %

Source: Adapted from *Education and Work*, Table V.

Table 20
ESTIMATED LENGTH OF PEL DAYS ATTENDANCE PER STUDENT
(SURVEY DATA)

Provider	Average Length of Course Estimated
Courses in educational institutions	17 — 4 days
Courses provided by management centres, etc.	5 — 3 days
Teachers centres	1 — 7 days
In-house provided by employers	6 days

Source: Adapted from *Education and Work*, Table VIII.

According to the Education and Work report, 45 per cent of the courses attended by 59 per cent of PEL students in educational institutions were without any qualification aim whatsoever. Furthermore, training provided by employers, teachers' centres and by private management colleges does not usually lead to any recognised qualification. Excluding degree courses, it appears that only about five per cent of those at educational institutions were on qualifying courses of a higher level standard. Looking at degree courses, the report comments in relation to England and Wales:

> "The number of undergraduates in receipt of PEL was probably in the range of 1000−2000 and could not have been greater than 2500 ... The number of post-graduate students (universities only) who were in attendance in the year 1976/77 and in receipt of PEL was probably in the region of 500" (43).

There are only two examples in Britain of legislation which explicitly confers the right to employees to claim paid leave to pursue certain courses of education. In the first case the Health and Safety at Work Act (1974) provides for the appointment of Health and Safety Representatives by trade unions. It is the duty of employers to liaise with these representatives on all matters relating to the health and safety of employees and to provide, at no cost to the employees, relevant information, instruction and training on these issues. Under the Regulations on Safety Representatives and Safety Committees (SL 1977 No. 500) an employer is obliged to permit the Safety Representative to take time off with pay during the employee's working hours to undertake training relevant to his responsibilities.

The second example where PEL is conferred as a right is the Employment Protection Act 1975 (consolidated 1978). It provides for recognised trade union officials to take time off during working hours for a variety of reasons, in particular, for purposes of training in aspects of industrial relations relevant to the carrying out of those duties, which are approved by the Trade Union Congress or the independent trade union of which he or she is an official.

As has already been mentioned, the Department of Education and Science and the Manpower Services Commission have initiated a number of pump-priming schemes such as Professional, Industrial and Commercial Updating (PICKUP) and Local Collaborative Projects which are designed on the one hand to assist universities and polytechnics to respond more efficiently to the training and education needs of employers, while on the other hand highlighting to employers the need to invest in the updating and retraining of their workforce. In addition the Department of Trade and Industry published a series of reports over the period 1984/5 which drew the attention of both employers and trainers to the problems related to growing skill shortages in the information technology areas, thus urging employers and other interested parties to pay much greater attention to continuing education of the workforce (44).

10. Summary

In attempting to put an overall figure to the extent of continuing education, it is useful to draw on the Advisory Council's work:

> "... it might seem that the numbers question could be reasonably answered by summing the number of participants in the principal sectors of education and training. Adding together the numbers released from industry to those in the public and independent further education sector, in the Responsible Bodies, and in some of the better known voluntary bodies, would give a figure approaching 20 per cent of the adult population. This would be misleading because of the large element of double counting; how many people engage in two or more educational activities at the same time? At least one-third of those released from work (probably at least a million) attend outside educational establishments and they would be double counted by any sum of participation rates from both sources. Allowing for double counting, the numbers of adults engaged in any one year is more likely *to be about 16 per cent of the adult population giving a figure of about six million in England and Wales"* (45).

Given the difference between an annual figure and one taken at a particular point in time, this figure of 16 per cent probably is generally given some support by the findings of a recent survey in England and Wales (46). Ten per cent of the respondents in this study were engaged in some form of continuing education and training at the time of the study and a further ten per cent had participated within the last three years. Fifty-one per cent had not undertaken any kind of education or training since completing their initial education.

B. CHARACTERISTICS OF STUDENTS ON CONTINUING EDUCATION PROGRAMMES

Unfortunately, the available statistics on this area are even more sketchy than for mature students on degree level courses. Much of the discussion therefore draws on findings of the survey already quoted of adults in education (47). One of the striking differences of adults on non-vocational, non-qualifying programmes is the representation of women. Whereas women were in the minority on degree programmes, they constitute approximately 77 per cent of the participants on non-vocational continuing education. As has been seen, the situation is however quite different when it comes to vocational education sponsored by employers, where women are again in the minority.

Tables 21 to 24 present data on the characteristics of adults attending courses which do not lead to a qualification provided by local education authorities through their adult education centres (LEA), by the Workers Educational Association (WEA) and by university extra-mural departments (EMD). It is important to note that these constitute the main providers of general, liberal adult education activities, but that few of their students are engaged in vocational updating or retraining. While there is a good deal of overlap in terms of the types of courses provided, by and large the LEA's offer more practically oriented courses (including hobby style courses) while, the WEA and extra-mural departments tend to offer more theoretical and academic types of programmes.

1. Educational background

Table 21 shows the educational background of adults involved in the three areas of provision. While these courses do not require any formal qualification on entry, only 12 per cent of those attending extra-mural courses in fact had no formal qualifications, with about one-quarter of those attending adult education centres falling into this category. Obviously these findings support those of other countries, where in general it is those who have already benefited from education who are the most likely to return as adults.

Table 21
HIGHEST EDUCATIONAL QUALIFICATION OF STUDENTS (25+)
IN CONTINUING EDUCATION (SURVEY DATA, PERCENTAGES)

Educational Level	LEA	WEA	EMD
No formal qualifications	25	17	12
'O' level or equivalent	33	26	23
'A' level or equivalent	10	20	18
Above 'A' level	32	37	47

Source: Mature Students Research Project

2. Employment Status

These differences are to some extent reflected in the class distribution of students at the different types of institutions. As Table 22 shows, students on LEA courses were twice as likely to be in lower service or manual positions than those on EMD courses. On the other hand, 61 per cent of the latter as opposed to only 46 per cent of the former were from the professional and higher service grouping.

Table 22
OCCUPATIONAL GROUPING OF STUDENTS (25+) IN CONTINUING
EDUCATION (SURVEY DATA, PERCENTAGES)

Occupational Grouping	LEA	WEA	EMD	Weighted Total
Professional and service	46	53	61	47
Other non-manual	40	31	31	39
Manual	15	16	8	14

Source: Mature Students Research Project

As Table 23 shows, about half of those at LEA and EMD courses were in employment with slightly fewer (40 per cent) of those from the WEA being in this category. Between a fifth and a quarter described themselves as housewives, and, while a fairly high proportion of all students were retired, this group were particularly noticeable in WEA courses.

Table 23
EMPLOYMENT STATUS OF STUDENTS (25+) IN CONTINUING EDUCATION (SURVEY DATA, PERCENTAGES)

	LEA	WEA	EMD
In paid employment			
(Full or part-time)	53	40	48
Not in paid employment			
Full-time housekeeper	26	21	25
Retired	18	36	20
Unemployed	1	1	1
Student	1	0	3
Other (e.g. disabled)	1	1	2
	47	*59*	*51*
Total	100	99	99

3. *Field of study*

Table 24 shows the subject areas of respondents (as has been pointed out previously, all students were on non-qualifying courses). The types of courses attended by respondents show the differences in provision between the three types of providers. EMDs and the WEA respondents were more likely to have attended artistic, aesthetic, social science and humanities courses than those at LEA classes, who were more likely to have attended physical, personal care or household economy courses.

Table 24
SUBJECT AREA OF STUDENTS (25+) IN CONTINUING EDUCATION (SURVEY DATA, PERCENTAGES)

Subject Area	LEA	WEA	EMD
Personal care/household economy	21	0	0
Artistic and aesthetic	17	40	28
Crafts	10	0	0
Physical skills/games	24	8	0
Scientific	1	1	18
Languages	15	4	6
Social sciences/humanities	5	44	41
Other (vocational, disadvantaged)	6	2	6

Source: Mature Students Research Project

C. CONTINUING EDUCATION: PROGRAMMES AND POLICIES OF UNIVERSITIES, POLYTECHNICS AND THE OPEN UNIVERSITY

1. *Universities*

The universities play a role in continuing education in two main ways. Firstly, through the work of their extra-mural departments, working either alone or jointly with the WEA; and secondly, through the continuing education work of intra-mural departments in the area of professional updating — particularly in the area of medicine. Table 25 shows the numbers of continuing education courses provided by universities through three main channels. Firstly, there are post-experience vocational education courses provided by internal university departments; secondly, post-graduate courses in the medical professions, and thirdly, the extra-mural courses already referred to in the previous section.

The background of the extra-mural tradition in Britain lies in the liberal concept of non-vocational adult education. Much of their current work is still in this vein with tutorial classes operating in the humanities and social sciences. On the other hand they have responded to changing circumstances by increasingly providing some form of certification of their courses and by offering business and professional updating courses.

In general, therefore, extra-mural departments provide a whole range of courses leading to certificates and diplomas, professional training, specialised group work in role education, post-experience refresher courses and in-service training. These take place alongside the traditional liberal non-qualifying courses provided by the extra-mural departments. The form of organisation varies between one-day seminars to tutorial classes comprised of three sessions of 24 meetings.

Table 25
NUMBER OF STUDENTS ON CONTINUING EDUCATION PROGRAMMES IN UNIVERSITIES

	1978/79	*1979/80*	*1980/81*	*1981/82*
Post-experience vocational education	80 907	83 355	85 734	105 331
Post-graduate medical and dental	56 662	68 223	74 716	84 778
Extra-mural	229 611	230 454	238 988	252 874
Totals	367 180	382 032	399 438	442 983

Source: UGC Report of the Continuing Education Working Party. Adapted from Appendix 8. Refers to Great Britain.

The figures in Table 25 reveal some very interesting trends. In 1978/79 extra-mural students represented 62 per cent of the total, while by 1981/82 this figure had dropped to 57 per cent. Over this period the numbers of students participating in these more general education programmes increased by 10 per cent, whereas over the same period the students engaging in professional updating increased much more dramatically. Adults on post-experience professional programmes increased by 30 per cent, while those on medical programmes increased by almost 50 per cent. There seems little doubt that this is a trend which is likely to continue in the future. The UGC report on continuing education makes clear that it sees this aspect of the work as being central if the universities are to respond to the dramatic changes in all areas of life and work expected as a result of the application of information technology and advances such as those in biotechnology, materials science and fibre optics.

The report does acknowledge that there are academic, organisational and financial problems to be overcome, and particularly comments that:

> One of the reasons why continuing education has remained a secondary activity in many universities is that responsibility for its constitutent parts has been dispersed (48).

A strong case is made for the establishment of an acknowledged focus of responsibility for continuing education commanding respect within the university and acting as the natural point of contact for outside bodies, in particular employers seeking assistance with the identification and ways of meeting their updating requirements.

In relation to the financing of these activities, it is government policy that the beneficiaries — and not the state — should meet the full costs involved. It is also UGC policy to encourage universities to seek to augment their income from external sources, the provision of professional continuing education being looked to as one way of generating additional income for institutions.

2. Polytechnics

It is difficult to document the work of polytechnics in the area of continuing education because so much of their work can be defined in this way. Many of the points covered in Chapter I would thus apply directly to this section also. This is partly due to the fact that they are the main higher education providers of part-time courses — some of which are simply short-cycle courses, while others form the basis of professional qualifications. The other factor is that the polytechnics were to some extent designed to develop close links with industry and business so their mainstream undergraduate provision has an almost natural spillover into continuing education.

Because of these traditional links between polytechnics and local employers, the bulk of their short course provision tends to be in the form of tailor-made programmes (often provided on-site) for industry, commerce and the professions. The method of organisation for this work varies considerably from institution to institution although the trend appears to be towards centralised support services.

A series of recommendations designed to foster continuing education in polytechnics and other public sector higher education institutions emerged from the 1984 report of the NAB Working Party on Continuing Education. These covered issues such as institutional attitudes and procedures, course structures, content and delivery, finance and student support. As with the UGC report the key element was the need for recognition of this area of work as a central function of institutions of higher education.

In relation to the distribution of students on short course continuing education programmes, there is a lack of accurate centralised statistics. The NAB report estimated that in 1983 approximately one-third of these adults were enrolled on courses in administration and business, with about one-eighth each in engineering, science, mathematics and education.

3. Open University

The Open University's continuing education (or associate student) programme is designed primarily for adults who have had practical experience in a given field and wish to develop or broaden their skills and understanding to a higher level. The courses selected for inclusion in the programme are considered to satisfy this need. The programme includes courses lasting about a year which were originally introduced as undergraduate courses; there are a number of other courses designed for certain professional areas, such as health and social welfare and in-service training for teachers; and there are at present a few courses, but with many more in the planning stage, designed to provide for professional, industrial and commercial updating needs.

In most cases associate (continuing education) students will be working towards either of two kinds of certification:

a) A Course Certificate of the Open University, obtained by a student who satisfactorily completes the course work required both in terms of continuous assessment and the examination. Course Certificates awarded for courses which are also offered in the undergraduate programme are the direct equivalent of Credit Certificates;

b) A Letter of Course Completion, obtained by a student who satisfactorily completes the course work required in terms of continuous assessment, but whose work is not formally examined. For most associate student courses, attendance at the examination is optional.

The majority of associate students study only one course with the Open University although there is an increasing trend for students to re-apply in a subsequent year to take another associate student course, again on a "one-off" basis.

D. COSTS AND FINANCING OF CONTINUING EDUCATION COURSES

1. Expenditure

If it is difficult to provide information on student numbers in adult and continuing education, it is generally recognised as next to impossible to provide more than estimates of the national expenditure on such diversified provision. Appendix 1 represents attempts to provide such estimates for England and Wales respectively. The expenditure figures are net of fees and other income and it is not possible to estimate how much of this was from public or private sources. It is also pointed out that it is not possible to estimate how much additional private funds, for example, from industry or commerce might have been devoted to the education of adults.

Table 26 attempts to approach the financing question from a different point of view. It shows that about 15 per cent of all education expenditure goes to non-initial education. This figure, however, does not distinguish by age, which the second column attempts to do. As the Advisory Council points out, even basing their figure on an estimate of 20 per cent going to those aged 25 or over, it shows a relatively small commitment of public money.

Table 26

PERCENTAGE OF ALL PUBLIC SECTOR EDUCATION EXPENDITURE SPENT ON THOSE OUTSIDE THE SCHOOL SYSTEM (1)

	Percentage of all Expenditure	Estimated Percentage on Adults 25+ (2)
Universities	3.0	
Advanced Further Education	2.0	
Non-Advanced Further Education	1.5	2.5
Student Awards	3.0	
All Further Education	3.0	
Open University; University Continuing Education	1.5	1.5
Adult Education (including responsible bodies)	1.0	1.0
TOTAL	*15.0*	*5.0*

1. Adapted from Table 19, *Continuing Education* (ACACE).
2. Based on the likely overestimate of 20 per cent being apportioned to those over 25 (see Chapter I, Table 1).

2. Fees

There is no centralised information available on fee structures and fee income. Appendix 2 gives an example from one important area of continuing education, namely, that provided by the extra-mural departments and the WEA. According to these figures income from fees constitutes eleven per cent of all income.

As much of this work is likely to have a non-vocational emphasis and therefore to be in the cheaper end of the fee spectrum, it is likey that fee income constitutes a more important component in the area of professional continuing education.

In fact, while there are many reasons behind the growth in continuing education courses for various professional groups, including moves towards increasing specialisation of provision and requests from the professions themselves, for help with updating, a further, not insignificant consideration is that in a time of financial constraint, experimenting with non-grant aided courses for such groups can be one means of avoiding stagnation if not actual contraction.

Certainly universities and polytechnics (and other public sector institutions) have in recent years been directed to charge for post-experience vocational education provision on a full-cost basis.

CONCLUSIONS

This paper has attempted an overview of the patterns and trends of participation by adults in higher education in the U.K. As was stated in the Introduction to Chapter 1, this is a difficult exercise, partly because of definitional problems and an absence of comprehensive statistics, but also because of the rapid rate of change in this area — particularly in relation to the involvement of universities, polytechnics and the Open University in vocational and professional updating and retraining. There is no doubt that at a national level policy makers in both university and public sector higher education are currently urging institutions to place continuing education on a par with their traditional functions of the teaching of young undergraduates and research. The Government paper on the "Development of Higher Education into the 1990s" published in May 1985 agreed with the University Grants Committee and the National Advisory Body for Public Sector Higher Education

> "... that the provision of continuing education should be one of the principal parts of higher education's work." (49)

The reasons for this increasing attention to widening access to adults to the resources of higher education are common to most OECD countries — firstly, there is the decline in the traditional age group which will not only have an impact on student numbers for institutions of higher education, but will also result in a shortage of graduates to take up the predicted expansion in professional, scientific and engineering occupations; however, it is also clear that the pace of scientific, technological and economic change will make demands on institutions to respond quickly and efficiently to updating, refreshing and re-orientation needs. As the National Advisory Body report points out, these needs are not just to do with technological advance but are also to do with changes in legislative and regulatory frameworks, changing social environments, changing patterns of work organisation and the creation of whole new fields of employment. The question of equality of opportunity is also a vital aspect of the case for continuing education, creating opportunities in higher education for women, for those from ethnic minorities, the unemployed and the "second chance" students.

In addressing the various elements of continuing education the NAB Working Party on Continuing Education refer to the importance of not stressing one aspect at the expense of another. As they say,

> "... there is no dilemma between meeting the needs of the economy for a more skilled and highly educated workforce responding to technological, economic and social change, the needs of society for harmonious responses to change and the aspiration of individuals for personal enjoyment, satisfaction and development. Rather these triple objectives must be seen as mutually reinforcing elements of a coherent strategy of increased support for continuing education; the benefits which will flow from an investment in continuing education should not be sacrificed for the comparatively small sums of expenditure which will bring them about." (50)

ABBREVIATIONS

AFE	Advanced Further Education
ACACE	Advisory Council on Adult and Continuing Education
BBC	British Broadcasting Corporation
CNAA	Council for National Academic Awards
DES	Department of Education and Science
EMD	University Extra-mural Department
GCE	General Certificate of Education (awarded at Ordinary ("O") Level and Advanced ("A") Level)
HE	Higher Education
LCP	Local Collaborative Project (DES and MSC initiative)
LEA	Local Education Authority
MSC	Manpower Services Commission
NAB	National Advisory Body for Public Sector Higher Education
NAFE	Non-Advanced Further Education
OU	Open University
PCAS	Polytechnic Central Admissions System
PEL	Paid Educational Leave
PICKUP	Professional, Industrial and Commercial Updating (DES initiative)
TOPS	Training Opportunities Scheme
UCCA	Universities' Central Council on Admissions
UDACE	Unit for the Development of Adult and Continuing Education
UGC	University Grants Committee
WEA	Workers Educational Association

NOTES AND REFERENCES

1. Universities Grants Committee (1984), *Report of the Continuing Education Working Party.*
   National Advisory Body for Public Sector Higher Education (1984), *Report of the Continuing Education Group.*
2. Approximately half of the students on advanced courses in the public sector are on undergraduate or post-graduate courses, with the remainder being divided between those on professional or sub-degree courses — D.E.S. *Part-Time Advanced Further Education* (1985).
3. Three at advanced level in Scotland.
4. *Report of the Mature Student Project* (1984) presented to the Department of Education and Science. This research was undertaken for the D.E.S. by a multi-disciplinary team based at the Open University, the Polytechnic of Central London and Lancaster University. The data has been re-analysed for purposes of this report. The survey covered adults attending courses at universities, polytechnics and other public sector institutions of higher education and the Open University. It also included adults on shorter courses not leading to qualifications. A. Woodley, L. Wagner, M. Slowey, M. Hamilton, O. Fulton (1987) *Choosing to Learn — Adults in Education*
5. Based on a sample of mature students at nine universities (including three College of the University of London).
6. Associate Students were not included.
7. Based on a sample of mature students at 44 public sector institutions of further and higher education.
8. Council for National Academic Awards (1980), *Annual Report.*
9. Council for National Academic Awards (1980), *Extension of Access to Higher Education.* Unpublished paper.
10. Advisory Council for Adult and Continuing Education (1979), *Adult Students and Higher Education.*
11. Unpublished statistics from the Universities Statistical Record.
12. Advisory Council for Adult and Continuing Education (1982), *Continuing Education From Policies to Practice*, p. 94.
13. *Ibid.*
14. *Adult Students and Higher Education, op. cit.*
15. D.E.S. (1983) *Educational Counselling and Credit Transfer Information Service.*
16. D.E.S. (1973) *Adult Education A Plan for Development* (the "Russell Report").
17. P. Toyne (1979) *Educational Credit Transfer Feasibility Study* — Exeter University.
18. D.E.S. (1983) *Educational Counselling and Credit Transfer Information Service.*
19. *Continuing Education, op. cit.* p. 93.
20. M. Tight (1982) *Part-Time Degree Level Study in the United Kingdom*, ACACE, p. 15.
21. *Ibid.*
22. The work of the extra-mural departments is discussed in more detail in Chapter 2.
23. Advisory Council for Adult and Continuing Education (1979), *Links to Learning.*
24. Advisory Council for Adult and Continuing Education (1981), *Directory of Educational Guidance Service for Adults.*
25. *Continuing Education, op. cit.*, p. 141.
26. D.E.S. (1978) *Higher Education in the 1980s*, p. 8. To some extent this view is echoed in the recent Government paper *The Development of Higher Education into the 1990s* (1985), which accepts the main proposals of the 1984 NAB and UGC reports on continuing education.
27. O. Fulton, Ed. (1981) *Access to Higher Education*, SRHE, p. 26.

28. G. Squires, "Mature Entry" in *Access to Higher Education, op. cit.*
29. J. Kileen and M. Bird (1981) *Education and Work — A Study of Paid Educational Leave,* NIAE, p. 95.
30. N. McIntosh and M. Rigg (1979) *Employers and the Open University*
31. B. Swift (1979) *Satisfied Expanded Happier — and Maybe Practical As Well,* O.U. Outlook No. 4.
32. *Mature Entry, op. cit.,* p. 167.
33. *Adult Education, op. cit.*
34. Advisory Council for Adult and Continuing Education (1979), *Towards Continuing Education*
35. D.E.S. (1980) *Continuing Education Post Experience Provision for Those in Employment.*
36. Advisory Council for Adult and Continuing Education (1980), *Present Imperfect.*
37. Manpower Services Commission (1981), *An Open Tech Programme*
38. *Education and Work, op. cit.*
39. *Ibid.,* p. 7.
40. As the authors point out, it is always "with reluctance" that a researcher mixes good statistics with the bad but sometimes it is necessary to do so to obtain overall estimations.
41. *Ibid.,* p. 7.
42. *Ibid.,* p. 42.
43. *Ibid.,* p. 27.
44. Department of Trade and Industry, IT Skills Committee Reports, (a) The *Human Factor — The Supply Side Problem* (1984); (b) *Changing Skills* (1985; (c) *Signposts for the Future* (1985).
45. *Continuing Education, op. cit.,* p. 46. Emphasis added.
46. Advisory Council for Adult and Continuing Education (1982), *Adult Students Their Educational Experience and Needs.*
47. See Footnote 4 and Chapter 1, Section B, for a description of this research project.
48. *Report of Continuing Education Working Party UGC, op. cit.,* p. 17.
49. *The Development of Higher Education into the 1990s, op. cit.,* p. 17.
50. *Report of Continuing Education Group, op. cit.,* p. 28.

APPENDIX 1
WALES: EXPENDITURE ON "ADULT" EDUCATION 1977-81
WITHIN THE EDUCATION SYSTEM

	1976/77	1977/78	£m 1978/79	1979/80	1980/81
Expenditure by local authorities	11.7	11.7	12.7	14.7	15.7
Adult education other than by local authorities	0.6	0.7	0.8	0.9	1.1
Student support	0.3	0.4	0.6	0.8	0.8
Total including student support	*12.6*	*12.8*	*14.1*	*16.4*	*17.6*

Source: 1. Figures supplied by D.E.S.

EXPENDITURE ON TRAINING BY THE MANPOWER SERVICES COMMISSION'S TRAINING SERVICES DIVISION (TSD)

	1976/77	1977/78	£m 1978/79	1979/80	1980/81
Helping to meet the training needs of the industry	68.2	90	99.2	97.7	99.7
Training Opportunities Scheme	182.9	194.0	204.4	226.2	247.6
Improving training effectiveness and efficiency	0.7	0.9	1.2	1.8	2.6
Management of TSD	7.8	7.0	7.7	3.5	Not available

1. *Source*: M.S.C. statistics.

ENGLAND: EXPENDITURE ON "ADULT" EDUCATION 1977-1981 WITHIN THE EDUCATION SYSTEM

	1976/77	1977/78	£m 1978/79	1979/80	1980/81
Expenditure by local authorities on education for "adults" (1) (2) (3)	234	241	269	312	382
Specific grants by Central Government (9)	5	6	7	8	11
University recurrent expenditure on adults (4) (5) (6)	107	99	110	133	172
Adult education other than local authorities (7) (3)	5	5	5	8	9
Open University	24	24	30	37	47
Teacher training (3)	9	8	7	8	11
Trade union studies	0.4	0.6	0.4	2.1	1.7
Total Excluding Study Support	*379*	*378*	*422*	*500*	*623*
Student support (3) (8) — mandatory and discretionary awards	35	52	60	69	85
Total Including Student Support	*420*	*436*	*489*	*577*	*719*

1. Includes advanced further education expenditure for students over 25, not advanced further education for students over 21, and adult education expenditure.
2. Net of tuition fee income.
3. England only expenditure figures.

4. 18 per cent of total universities recurrent expenditure on basis of number of students over 25.
5. Includes the same proportion of Computer Board expenditure.
6. Great Britain expenditure figures.
7. Central Government grants to Workers' Educational Association, extra-mural departments of universities, long-term residential colleges and national bodies.
8. Assuming 12 per cent of mandatory and discretionary awards expenditure is to people over 25.
9. Under special programmes, for example, certain LEAs can obtain 75 per cent reimbursement from the Home Office for salaries related to programmes for Commonwealth immigrants, and 75 per cent reimbursement from the Department of the Environment for projects in urban areas of special social need.

Source: Based on DES response to UNESCO's questionnaire on adult education (1982).

APPENDIX 2
INCOME AND EXPENDITURE OF RESPONSIBLE BODIES
(UNIVERSITY EXTRA-MURAL DEPARTMENTS AND THE WORKERS EDUCATIONAL ASSOCIATION) IN ENGLAND AND WALES, 1979

	£'000s	
Expenditure:		
Grant-Aided Teaching Costs		
Full-time tutors	4 895	
Part-time tutors	2 402	
Non-Grant Aided Teaching Costs	*1 305*	
Administrative and Other	*3 799*	Total: 12 401
Income:		
Fees	1 362	
DES Grant	5 532	
LEA	560	
Universities	306	
WEA	1 177	Total: 12 294
Excess of expenditure over income:	107	

Source: Adapted from Table D9(9), *Statistics on Finance and Awards 1980*, DES, 1980.

Adults in higher education:
The situation in the United States

by
Alan P. Wagner

TABLE OF CONTENTS

Page

Chapter I: Adults in Higher Education — The Framework
A. The Environment for Adult Participation in Higher and
   Further (Continuing) Education in the 1980s   79
B. An Overview of the Structure, Finance, and Governance
   of Higher and Further (Continuing) Education
   in the United States   81
   1. Structure   82
   2. Programmes   82
   3. Governance   82
   4. Trends   84
   5. Finances   86
C. Trends and Characteristics of Adults in Higher and Further
   (Continuing) Education   87
   1. Trends in Educational Attainment by Age, Sex, and Labour
      Force Status   87
   2. Patterns of Participation by Age, Sex, Labour Force Status,
      and Programme   89
D. Policies Affecting Adult Participation in Higher and Further
   (Continuing) Education   92

Chapter II: Degree-Credit Higher Education   93
A. Financing   93
   1. Institutional Financial Support   93
   2. Student Financial Support   95
      a. Grants   96
      b. Entitlements   98
      c. Loans   99
      d. Private Sources   100
   3. Tax Expenditures   101
B. Admissions and Crediting   101
C. Non-Traditional Attendance Options   103
D. New Institutions and Providers   105
E. Student Support Services   107

	Page
Chapter III: Further (Continuing) Education	109
A. Financing	109
1. Public Institutional Financial Support	109
2. Student Financial Support	110
3. Tax Expenditures	111
B. New Providers	111
Conclusions	114
A. Institutional Responses to Pressures and Policies:	114
B. Public Policy Impacts	115
Notes	116
References	117

Chapter I
Adults in higher educations
The framework

A. THE ENVIRONMENT FOR ADULT PARTICIPATION IN HIGHER AND FURTHER (CONTINUING) EDUCATION IN THE 1980s

The growing participation of adults in a wide variety of post-compulsory education and training activities has been heralded as the beginning of a new era of challenges and opportunities for institutions of higher education. Adults represent a large, exciting, new clientele for institutions sorely in need of an infusion of students and resources. At the same time, for colleges and universities accustomed to serving a captive, relatively homogeneous younger student group, the educational demands of adults pose difficult problems for how existing or new resources are to be used.

This paper reports on the extent and patterns of adult participation in programmes of higher and further (continuing) education in the United States. Beyond describing the volume and nature of the involvement, the paper presents an evaluation of the effects of selected public policy, private, and institutional initiatives on adult participation. Institutions of higher education, encouraged by public policy pressures, are beginning to respond to the burgeoning adult enrollment demands. But, while the policies and programmes of institutions, as well as those of federal, state, and local governments, are not intended to exclude adults from higher and further education, many have operated to make adult participation difficult or less attractive.

For the purposes of the paper, "adults" are defined to include those 25 years of age or older. Within the adult population, we shall be particularly concerned with the enrollments of those who have not completed a higher education course of study. Post-secondary educational providers of instruction consist of "institutions of higher education," comprised largely of traditional colleges and universities, and "non-collegiate post-secondary schools." The latter group includes technical and vocational institutes, organized to provide occupational and vocational skill training.

The numbers are impressive: thirty three million adults, 25 years of age and older, participated in at least one organized post-high school learning activity in 1983. About 7 million of the total received instruction through one or more programmes offered at institutions of higher education; non-collegiate post-secondary institutions provided training for another 600 thousand (updated from Wagner 1983b). These numbers represent large increases in adult participation in post-secondary education and training from 1970 levels. And, due to a number of demographic, economic, social, and policy influences, most believe the participation of adults in post-compulsory education and training will continue to grow in the last half of the decade.

First, the aging of the relatively large post-World War II birth cohorts, alone, would imply growing numbers of potential adult students.

Secondly, however, the United States economy is continuing to experience wrenching financial and technological changes that will require quite different skill mixes. With the adoption of new technologies during the 1982-84 economic recovery, firms are seeking workers with newer skills. But, many believe the supply of workers embodied with the new skills will be inadequate to meet the demands (Nollen 1984; Wagner 1984). As a result, large numbers of employed and displaced adults are likely to require training at all levels. Importantly, the needs for retraining surfacing in the early 1980s may well persist, as new technologies continue to be introduced and adopted at increasingly rapid rates. Workers and employers might find the best strategy for the timing of education would call for later and periodic training geared to specific skills. The current structure, focussed as it is on a single period of education followed by a long period of work, accommodates primarily the younger participants.

Thirdly, stimulated by the growth in female-headed households and a strong market for female college graduates in a variety of fields, the steady and pronounced increases in female labor force participation rates for women of all ages suggests an additional source of current and future growth in the demand for higher and further education.

Finally, we have a growing policy interest in the education and training of adults — including their participation in higher and further education. The interest flows, in part, from a renewed emphasis on productivity and national security. As the United States economy continues its recovery from the 1981-82 recession, the Reagan administration has put forth limited "supply side" proposals to promote economic growth through expanding the productive capacities of the nation's resources. Moreover, the current and anticipated skill shortages have also been viewed as an alarming potential threat to national security. Quite apart from the weaknesses introduced in the general economy by skill shortages, defense experts doubt that sufficient numbers of skilled workers and armed forces personnel will be available to develop, maintain, and operate the increasingly sophisticated array of equipment and armaments. These pressures have led some to recommend a new large training effort, similar to the 1958 National Defense Education Act, to upgrade and maintain the skill levels of the workforce and armed forces in order to ensure a strong economy and a strong defense.

The policy interest extends to concerns about ensuring opportunity for females, minorities, and low income/unemployed populations. In this area, public intervention to promote the participation of adults may be seen as a "corrective" for low prior educational attainment.

Against these sources of potential growth in adult post-compulsory education and training, several countervailing forces may work to limit participation in programmes offered by institutions of higher education. First, whether higher and further education still "pays" for participants, employers, and the public remains an issue. When supplies of trained manpower exceed demands in some fields, some speak of retreating from a position of "overexpansion" of higher and further education (Rumberger 1984). Second, institutions of higher education face a growing array of competitors for adult students. Particularly in the popular professional programmes, adults have more training options, and their usual sources of financing provide support for training in non-collegiate as well as higher education programmes. Public policy makers are even considering whether public sources of support, including student financial aid, should be available to participants in effective and comparable non-school programmes of higher and further education and training. Third, budget pressures within institutions, states, and at the federal level now limit the potential for financing *new* innovations. In the current environment, decision makers at all levels may need to reduce some existing activities if they wish to start, or expand, programmes available principally to adults.

With these sets of pressures as backdrop, we begin with an overview of the system of higher and further education in the United States.

B. AN OVERVIEW OF THE STRUCTURE, FINANCE, AND GOVERNANCE OF HIGHER AND FURTHER (CONTINUING) EDUCATION IN THE UNITED STATES

Post-secondary education represents a major investment in the productive capacities of the population in the United States. By 1983, more than two-thirds of the population 25 years old and over had graduated from high school, with half of the high school graduates completing at least one year of higher education (U.S. Department of Labor 1984). Even recognizing that the first two years of higher education in the United States correspond to upper-secondary schooling in the European system, the numbers involved suggest a system of mass higher education.

In 1983-84, over 3 000 institutions of higher education provided instruction for over 19 million students in courses creditable toward a post-secondary certificate or higher education degree, or in non-credit activities (updated from Wagner 1983b). These aggregate numbers hide much of the diversity in United States higher education. Details on its structure, programmes, governance, and finance are provided in Tables 1 to 4. A few general comments, however, are in order.

1. Structure

Of the 3 284 institutions of higher education in the United States, about three-fifths (1 894) are four-year colleges and universities, offering courses to the baccalaureate degree or beyond. According to data reported for the fall of 1983, these institutions enrolled about three-fifths of the 9.7 million students engaged in undergraduate degree-creditable courses (Table 1). Almost 1 300 two-year colleges provide instruction through the first two years of higher education, conferring associate degrees as recognition of the completion of a two-year, college creditable course of study. Students completing courses at two-year colleges may transfer into four-year institutions and proceed directly on to a baccaulaureate degree.

2. Programmes

Institutions of higher education do not limit their instructional activities to degree-creditable courses. As can be seen in Table 2, a large proportion of colleges and universities offer short-term, non-credit courses: an estimated 12.3 million registrations recorded in 1979-80 alone (1). Since many participants in these non-credit programmes enroll for more than one course, the registrations represent 5 to 6 million participants. Job-related courses attracted an estimated 8 million registrations, while courses responding to specific professional education needs accounted for 3.6 million registrations. Across institutional types, two-year colleges reported more than half of all registrations (6.7 million). However, universities and other four-year colleges account for larger shares of the job-related and professional education courses.

Institutions for higher education also offer a limited number of non-collegiate, primarily occupational courses. A 1982 survey revealed some 1 600 colleges and universities offered at least one technical programme, usually with a duration of one to two years, leading to a certificate of completion (Litkowski 1983b). While representing a relatively small share of the institutions offering these programmes, the higher education sector enrolled over half of non-collegiate students in 1982 (Hill 1985).

3. Governance

The public role in higher education in the United States is limited essentially to financing and regulatory matters, and rests primarily with state governments, rather than with the federal government or local jurisdictions. With the recent slowdown in federal research and education outlays and the severe restrictions placed on local public revenue sources through property tax limitation measures, the pre-eminence of the state role will continue.

Table 1
INSTITUTIONS AND ENROLLMENTS IN HIGHER EDUCATION: 1983-84

	Institutions		Undergraduate Enrollments	
	Number	*Percent*	*(000's)*	*Percent*
TOTAL	*3 284*	*100.0%*	*9 707*	*100.0%*
Doctoral	171	5.2	2 096	21.6
Comprehensive Four-Year	418	12.7	2 201	22.7
General Baccalaureate	710	21.6	988	10.2
Specialized	595	18.1	355	3.6
Two-Year	1 272	38.7	4 008	41.3
New	118	3.6	58	.6
PUBLIC	*1 481*	*45.1*	*7 733*	*80.0*
Doctoral	109	3.3	1 759	18.1
Comprehensive Four-Year	254	7.7	1 751	18.0
General Baccalaureate	118	3.6	326	3.4
Specialized	67	2.0	135	1.4
Two-Year	921	28.0	3 752	38.6
New	12	.	4 9	—
PRIVATE NON−PROFIT	*1 605*	*48.9*	*1 793*	*18.5*
Doctoral	62	1.9	337	3.5
Comprehensive Four-Year	164	5.0	450	4.6
General Baccalaureate	591	18.0	659	6.8
Specialized	208	6.3	200	2.1
Two-Year	515	15.7	137	1.4
New	65	2.0	10	.4
PRIVATE PROFIT−MAKING	*198*	*6.0*	*180*	*1.8*
Doctoral	—	—	—	—
Comprehensive Four-Year	—	—	—	—
General Baccalaureatel	—	—	3	—
Specialized	143	4.4	20	.2
Two-Year	13	.4	119	1.2
New	41	1.2	39	.4

Note: The institutional classifications convey the range and extent of programs. The first four categories distinguish principally among institutions with programs at the baccalaureate level and/or above. New institutions have become newly-eligible for inclusion in the universe of institutions of higher education; they will be assigned to one of the other categories as the numbers, fields, and academic levels of students and graduates become available.

Source: U.S. Department of Education, National Center for Education Statistics, *Education Directory 1983–84*, 1985b, Table 2; U.S. Department of Education, National Center for Education Statistics, *Fall Enrollment in Colleges and Universities 1983*, 1985c, Table 4A.

Institutions of higher education -- both public and private — exercise broad discretion in administering programmes and allocating available dollars. Public institutions differ from private and profit-making colleges and universities in the amount of public funds they receive to meet general operating expenses. Private and profit-making institutions finance their instructional programmes largely through tuition and gifts or endowment income. However, the distinction between public and private or profit-making is more a matter of degree. Public colleges receive part of their income from private sources (student tuition and private gifts), while private and profit-making institutions rely on some indirect federal, state and local support through tax exemptions and deductions (for institutions and students) and financial aid.

As the figures in Tables 1 and 2 indicate, the public, private, and profit-making sectors differ in size and enrollment composition. Public colleges, 60 per cent of which are two-year institutions, enroll about 7.7 million (or 80 per cent) of the first-degree students in higher education. With a comparable number of institutions, the private non-profit sector accounts for 1.8 million. Further, public colleges and universities provide most of the non-credit, continuing education activities in higher education. Almost 94 per cent of public institutions, compared to a little over half of the private colleges, offer non-credit courses. Public institutions accounted for 88 per cent of all non-credit registrations (10.8 million of the 12.3 million recorded), and over four-fifths of the registrations in professional education activities.

Not surprisingly, the states clearly influence the profile of higher education within their boundaries. The relative size of the public sector among selected states differs markedly, from about half of all institutions in California and Kansas to less than a third of all institutions in New York State. These differences mask the extent of each state's financial stake in higher education. Even with a relatively large private sector, New York provided subsidies to higher education averaging about $2,500 per student in 1984-85 (ACUSNY 1986).

4. Trends

Over time, enrollments have increased most rapidly at public institutions, principally at the two-year colleges. As the figures in Table 3 reveal, a slightly

Table 2

INSTITUTIONS AND REGISTRATIONS IN CONTINUING (FURTHER) EDUCATION: 1979–80

| | Institutions Offering | | Registrations | | | | | |
| | | | Total | | Job-Related[a] | | Professional[b] Education | |
	Number	as % of total in sector	(000's)	Percent	(000's)	Percent	(000's)	Percent
TOTAL	2,285	72.2 %	12,286	100.0 %	8,073	100.0 %	3,614	100.0 %
University	158	94.0	3,154	25.7	2,719	33.6	1,522	42.1
Other Four-Year	1,148	64.0	2,394	19.5	1,819	22.5	987	27.3
Two-Year	979	81.2	6,738	54.8	3,409	42.2	1,105	30.6
PUBLIC	1,394	93.7	10,832	88.2	6,931	85.8	2,936	81.2
University	98	100.0	2,370	19.3	2,030	25.1	1,082	29.9
Other Four-Year	410	91.1	1,760	14.3	1,445	17.9	766	21.2
Two-Year	886	94.3	6,701	54.5	3,449	42.7	1,088	30.1
PRIVATE	891	53.1	1,455	11.8	1,139	14.1	677	18.7
University	60	85.7	784	6.4	688	8.5	440	12.2
Other Four-Year	738	55.0	634	5.2	427	5.3	221	6.1
Two-Year	93	35.1	37	.3	23	.3	16	.4

[a] Excludes fine arts, home economics, letters, psychology, theology, developmental activites, physical education, and other avocational instruction, *except* registrations organized to meet professional education needs.

[b] Activities specifically developed to help members in a profession or occupation keep abreast of the latest developments in their field.

Source: R. Calvert, Jr., *Non-Credit Activities in Institutions of Higher Education for the Year Ending June 30, 1980, 1982.*

larger number of institutions accomodated part of the growth in degree-credit enrollments over the 1979 to 1983 period. In fact, most of the shift in the numbers of institutions represents colleges changing from the private to the public sector or technical institutes expanding their college-creditable course offerings, and being recognized as institutions of higher education.

Although information on non-credit enrollments at colleges and universities is not readily available, some fragmentary data from the Department of Education's Participation in Adult Education surveys suggests the rate of growth in non-credit enrollments has slowed considerably (U.S. Department of Education 1985d). The trend likely results from tighter pressures on college and university budgets along with increased competition for adult enrollments from non-college providers.

Table 3
CHANGES IN INSTITUTIONS AND PARTICIPANTS IN HIGHER EDUCATION: 1979-80 to 1983-84 Percent Change

	Undergraduate Institutions (1)		Enrollments	
	1979-80 to 1981-82	1981-82 to 1983-84	1979-80 to 1981-82	1981-82 to 1983-84
TOTAL	+ 3.2%	+ 1.0%	+ 7.7%	+ 2.1%
Four-Year	− 1.8	− .2		+ .8
Two-Year	− .3	+ 4.8		− .4
PUBLIC	+ 1.6%	− 1.1%	+ 7.5%	+2.2%
Four-Year	.0	− .4		+ 1.4
Two-Year	+ .9	- 1.3		+ 3.6
PRIVATE, TOTAL	+ 4.6%	+ 2.7%	+ 8.8%	+ 1.9%
Four-Year	− 2.5	− .1		- .6
Two-Year	− 4.0	+ 24.9		+ 39.1
PROFIT MAKING	+ 45.1%	+ 17.8%	+ 55.9%	+ 25.9%
Four-Year				+ 22.2
Two-Year				+ 91.9

(1). Includes newly eligible institutions not shown separately.

Sources: U.S. Department of Education, National Center for Education Statistics, *Education Directory 1983−84*, 1985b, Table 2 and unpublished tabulations; U.S. Department of Education, National Center for Education Statistics, *Fall Enrollment in Colleges and Universities 1983*, 1985c, Table 4A (and earlier volumes).

5. *Finances*

The costs of providing instruction at post-secondary educational institutions totaled an estimated $39.6 billion in 1980. This figure excludes the value of time students devoted to classes and study, an unmeasured opportunity cost. The estimates are shown in Table 4. In broad terms, perhaps one-half of four-year college instructional costs, and four-fifths of the instructional costs at two-year colleges, were financed — directly or indirectly — through public sources. A sizable portion of the costs of courses at institutions of higher education, however, are met by students and their families.

Note that these figures represent aggregate estimates, across programmes of study and states. For example, other data suggest that students enrolled in part-time or non-degree courses bear a large share of the direct costs of instruction than do those enrolled full-time, in degree-creditable courses (Wagner 1978b; Pitchell 1974).

C. TRENDS AND CHARACTERISTICS OF ADULTS IN HIGHER AND FURTHER CONTINUING) EDUCATION

That the system of higher education in the United States has expanded is evident from the increase in expenditures for higher education as well as the educational attainment of the population. However, differences in attainment and participation across age, sex, race, income, and labour force groups reveal the groups of adults who may benefit, or are benefitting, from additional higher and further education opportunities.

1. Trends in Educational Attainment by Age Sex and Labour Force Status
First, as shown in Table 5, mature age individuals have received less formal education than those from younger age groups. In 1983, 24 per cent of the 25 to 34 year old age cohort were college graduates; 18 per cent of 45 to 54 year olds had reached the same level. And, even though the latter share represents a significant gain since 1976, the improvement has occurred largely due to the aging of younger, better educated age cohorts rather than policies and the effects of programmes promoting adult participation in higher education. Moreover, the differences across age groups remain, even if narrowed over time.

A second interpretation of the figures points toward the nature of courses demanded by an increasingly better educated population. Given their higher levels of attainment, adults desiring courses as "deferrers", "refreshers," or "recyclers" will likely seek out offerings at a higher level than would have been true less than a decade ago.

Third, the improvement in educational attainment has narrowed, but not eliminated, the differences by sex. Within every age cohort, females have completed less college education than males: at 25 to 34 years, 26.8 per cent of the males compared to 22.1 per cent of the females have completed college. For 45 to 54 year olds, the difference is even greater (24.0 per cent versus 12.2 per cent).

87

Table 4
COSTS AND SOURCES OF FUNDS FOR POST-COMPULSORY EDUCATION AND TRAINING PROGRAMMES: 1980

| | COST OF IN-STRUCTION Millions of dollars | SOURCES OF FUNDS Millions of dollars | | | | | |
| | | Public Sources | | | Private Sources | | |
		Instit. Approp.	Student Aid Grants	Tax Expend.	Employer	Other	Student and/or Family
TOTAL	$39600	$18050	$4800	$1150	$375	$1500	$13775
Four-Year Institutions	24,525	10,300	2,900	1,050	200	1,400	8,675
Two-Year Institutions	5,675	3,925	850	50	75	50	775
Vocational Schools	4,300	3,450	600	25	50	25	150
Proprietary Schools	4,	275	400	25	50	25	3,275
Correspondence Schools	1,050	100	50	-	-	-	900

Institutional Appropriations include funds from federal, state, and local jurisdictions allocated to the provider.

Student Aid Grants include public grants and scholarships awarded directly to students, 50 percent of proceeds from federal loan programs (an estimate of the present value of implicit subsidies in the programs), and 25 percent of Veteran's Administration benefits (an estimate of the proportion of VA benefits covering tuition and

Tax Expenditures consist of reduced tax liabilities resulting from private tuition aid plans and corporate and individual support of educational and training programs.

Employer support includes amounts provided for tuition aid and on-site college programs, net of tax expenditures.

Other support includes corporate, non-profit, and individual support of education programs, either to institutions or to students (net of tax expenditures).

Student and/or Family includes funds provided by participants out of pocket or supported through proceeds from work or loans (net of implicit subsidy and tax expenditures). This is a residual.

Source: Wagner, "Post-Compulsory Education and Training: An Inventory of Programs and Sources of Support," in: *H. Levin and H.G. Schütze, (eds.), Financing Recurrent Education, op.cit., Table 3.*

Table 5
EDUCATIONAL ATTAINMENT OF THE POPULATION BY SEX AND
AGE: 1976 AND 1983

Sex and Age	Population (in thousands)		Percent High School Graduates only		Percent College Graduates	
	1976	1983	1976	1983	1976	1983
TOTAL						
25 to 34 years	31 148	38 938	41.5	40.1	22.6	24.4
35 to 44 years	22 819	28 690	41.7	40.1	16.6	23.5
45 to 54 years	23 452	22 176	39.9	41.6	12.7	13.6
55 to 64 years	19 767	21 985	34.5	38.5	9.8	13.6
MALE						
25 to 34 years	15 266	19 034	37.2	37.6	26.7	26.8
35 to 44 years	11 107	13 884	36.6	35.6	21.7	28.7
45 to 54 years	11 296	10 692	34.0	35.4	16.9	24.0
55 to 64 years	9 320	10 253	31.2	32.5	12.1	18.0
FEMALE						
25 to 34 years	15 877	19 904	45.6	42.4	18.6	22.1
35 to 44 years	11 712	14 675	46.6	44.0	11.8	19.0
45 to 54 years	12 156	11 484	45.5	47.3	8.8	12.2
55 to 64 years	10 477	11 732	37.6	43.8	7.7	9.8

Source: U.S. Department of Labor, Bureau of Labor Statistics, Educational Attainment of Workers, 1982-83, *Special Labor Force Report*, Bulletin 2191 (April 1984), Tables B-4 and B-6; Kopp Michelotti, Educational Attainment of Workers, March 1976, *Monthly Labor Review* 100 (March 1977): 62-65.

When this difference is linked to changing labour force participation rates, the case for attempting to improve the employment and income prospects of adult females through higher education becomes more compelling. As shown in Table 6, females are working or looking for work in increasing numbers. From 1976 to 1983, the share of 25 to 34 year old female high school graduates in the labour force rose from 54.6 to 66.3 per cent. Even mature age women, 45 to 54 years old, with college degrees are represented in greater numbers in the labour force (74.4 per cent compared to a 70.5 per cent labour force participation rate in 1976). The causes for increases in the labour force participation of adult women have been explored by others (Arbeiter, Aslanian, Schmerbeck, and Brickell 1978; Aslanian and Brickell 1980; Astin 1976); almost all could materially benefit from acquiring or updating their college level skills (2).

2. *Patterns of Participation by Age Sex Labour Force Status and Programme*
While the patterns of educational attainment show which adult groups might benefit from higher or further (continuing) education, the available participation data indicate a relatively low adult involvement in degree-credit higher education. According to data culled from recent Department of Education Surveys, those 25 years of age or older account for less than 13 per cent of all

full-time collegiate enrollments, but almost 80 per cent of part-time, non-degree enrollments at institutions of higher education (Table 7).

The data indicate adult females participate in all forms of undergraduate and further education programmes in greater numbers than adult males. For those 25 years old and over, 398 thousand females, compared to 394 thousand males, enrolled full-time. Among part-time undergraduate enrollees, females outnumber males by almost 200 thousand (1 057 thousand versus 883 thousand). And, nearly three of every five adult participants in non-credit courses are female (Table 7). This appears to be a reassuring finding, since adult females have received less prior education than their male counterparts. However, other data indicate that adult males tend to participate in greater numbers in graduate programmes and in programmes offered by providers other than colleges and universities (employers and professional associations, for example); these programmes serve to maintain the existing differences in education and training (Wagner 1983).

Table 6
LABOUR FORCE PARTICIPATION BY EDUCATIONAL ATTAINMENT SEX AND AGE: 1976 AND 1983

| Sex and Age | Labour Force Participation Rate for: | | | |
| | High School Graduates only | | College Graduates | |
	1976	1983	1976	1983
TOTAL				
25 to 34 years	75.0%	79.4%	80.5%	89.3%
35 to 44 years	75.2	81.6	87.8	89.3
45 to 54 years	73.3	75.9	85.8	88.1
55 to 64 years	59.1	54.5	71.4	72.9
MALE				
25 to 34 years	95.3%	94.9%	94.8%	95.2%
35 to 44 years	96.8	96.1	97.1	98.2
45 to 54 years	96.6	93.0	93.9	94.7
55 to 64 years	78.4	70.0	81.9	83.6
FEMALE				
25 to 34 years	54.6%	66.3%	71.3%	82.6%
35 to 44 years	59.2	70.6	71.8	76.5
45 to 54 years	57.1	64.0	70.5	74.4
55 to 64 years	44.9	44.4	57.5	56.0

Source: U.S. Department of Labor, Bureau of Labor Statistics, Educational Attainment of Workers, 1982-83, Special Labor Force Report, Bulletin 2191 (April 1984), Tables B-4 and B-6; Kopp Michelotti, Educational Attainment of Workers, March 1976, *Monthly Labor Review* 100 (March 1977): 62-65.

Table 7

PARTICIPATION IN HIGHER AND CONTINUING (FURTHER) EDUCA-TION BY SEX AND AGE: 1983-84

	Undergraduate Full-Time		Degree-Credit Part-Time		Non-Degree Credit Part-Time	
	(000s)	Percent	(000s)	Percent	(000s)	Percent
TOTAL	6 408	100.0%	3 183	100.0%	5 806	100.0%
17 to 24 years	5 616	87.6	1 243	39.0	1 251	21.6
25 years and over	792	12.4	1 940	61.0	4 555	78.4
MALE	3 280	100.0%	1 464	100.0%	2 466	100.0%
17 to 24 years	2 886	88.0	581	39.7	528	21.4
25 years and over	394	12.0	883	60.3	1 938	78.6
FEMALE	3 128	100.0%	1 719	100.0%	3 340	100.0%
17 to 24 years	2 730	87.2	662	38.5	723	21.6
25 years and over	398	12.8	1 057	61.5	2 617	78.4

Note: Numbers represent duplicated counts. Some participants enrolled in both degree-credit *and* non-credit programmes during the year.

Source: Estimated from U. S. Department of Education, *The Condition of Education 1985 Edition*, 1985a, Table 2.5; U.S. Department of Education, National Center for Education Statistics, *Projections of Education Statistics to 1992−93*, 1985e, Tables 8 and B-4A; U.S. Department of Education, National Center for Education Statistics, *Fall Enrollment in Colleges and Universities 1983*, 1985c, Table 4A; U.S. Department of Education, *Participation in Adult Education May 1984*, 1985d, unpublished tabulations.

Differences in other social and economic attributes among participants are shown in Table 8. The data refer to the 1981-82 period, the latest year for which detailed information is readily available. However, similar patterns would likely emerge from more recent data. As shown in Table 8, blacks and other minorities represent larger proportions of adult full-time enrollments than of adult part-time enrollments. And, in every form of participation, minority representation equals or exceeds their shares in the population. Those adults currently married with a spouse present account for more than two-fifths of full-time adult enrollments and nearly three-fifths of the adult part-time student pool (3).

With respect to incomes of adult participants, the available data indicate relatively larger proportions of full-time adult students are drawn from the lower ends of the income distribution, while just the opposite pattern obtains among adults enrolling part-time. Finally, employed adults comprise the largest shares of adults enrolled in higher education programmes. However, whereas only 11.1 per cent of part-time adult students were not in the labour force, fully 43.2 per cent of full-time adult students were neither working nor looking for work.

Whether institutions of higher education are best suited to provide education and training to adults most in need of it remains a hotly contested policy question. But, given the large public subsidies allocated to higher education and the quality and nature of the available programmes of instruction, the policies affecting the participation of adults in programmes at institutions of higher education would warrant a further examination.

D. POLICIES AFFECTING ADULT PARTICIPATION IN HIGHER AND FURTHER (CONTINUING) EDUCATION

What initiatives have been undertaken to promote the participation of adults in higher or further education? Have they been successful? The policies and practices considered below reflect changes in the financing and organisation of higher and further education. Not all of the changes were undertaken to promote the participation of adults. However, none of the policies and programmes intended to exclude them.

Chapter II
Degree-credit higher education

A. FINANCING

In the United States, the principal tool used to serve public policy interests —
whether at the national, state, or local level -is financing. Organisational
practices may, on occasion, be imposed as a matter of public policy, but more
often the public bodies affect these practices through financing (or a lack of it).
Public financing of higher education may be provided through the institutions,
directly to students, or indirectly to institutions, students or donors with tax
relief provisions.

1. *Institutional Financial Support*
Over the 1960s and 1970s, the large investment in the expansion of the higher
education system in the United States greatly expanded opportunities for
enrollments of adults. The growth in the number of campuses put a relatively
low cost institution of higher education within commuting distance for most
adults, and the effects on adult enrollments appear to have been dramatic and
are still continuing. While undergraduate enrollments grew by 11 per cent over
the 1978 to 1983 period, adult enrollments in undergraduate programmes
increased by 13 per cent overall, and by 27 per cent at community colleges
(estimated from U.S. Department of Education 1985e).

The growth in adult enrollments has occurred in spite of institutional tuition
and fee schedules which frequently impose charges closer to the full cost of
instruction for part-time attendance (the option most favoured by adults) than
for full-time attendance. An early 1970s review of tuition policies revealed that

over half of the institutions surveyed assessed higher tuition and fees per credit hour to their part-time students than to full-time students (Pitchell 1974). The situation has not changed significantly since then (4).

Table 8
CHARACTERISTICS OF ADULT PARTICIPANTS IN HIGHER EDUCATION: 1981-82

Characteristic	Adult Population Percent	Full-Time, Degree Credit Percent	Part-Time, Degree Credit Percent
TOTAL	100.0%	100.0%	100.0%
SEX			
Male	46.8%	47.0%	37.5%
Female	53.2	53.0	62.5
RACIAL/ETHNIC GROUP			
White	84.5%	79.0%	84.2%
Black	9.3	12.3	8.4
Other	6.2	8.7	7.4
MARITAL STATUS			
Married, spouse present	67.6%	41.0%	58.1%
Other Marital Status	32.4	59.0	41.9
INCOME			
Less than $7 500	19.4%	23.7%	10.8%
$7 500 to $14 999	22.8	24.8	23.0
$15 000 to $24 999	25.7	30.4	37.8
$25 000 and over	32.0	20.6	28.3
EMPLOYMENT STATUS			
Working	54.2%	52.9%	83.3%
Looking for work	2.2	3.9	5.6
Not in labour force	43.6	43.2	11.1

Source: Estimated from U.S. Department of Commerce, Bureau of the Census, "School Enrollment — Social and Economic Characteristics of Students: October 1981 and 1980," *Current Population Reports*, P-20, No. 400, 1985; U.S. Department of Education, National Center for Education Statistics, "Participation in Adult Education — May 1981," unpublished tabulations, 1983; Hill, "Participants in Postsecondary Education," *NCES Special Report* 84-809, 1985.

During the 1980's, as state appropriations for higher education have levelled in most states, and declined in several, public institutions have looked to higher tuition and fees to meet the shortfall. While tuition increases certainly discourage enrollments from all groups, the effects of the increases may well be greater on adult enrollments. The limited available research supports this view. Where tuition and fees for part-time attendance have been *reduced* through the allocation of general institutional subsidies, enrollments, including those of adults, have increased. In the mid-1970s, Northern Illinois University cut the per credit hour tuition to part-time students from $30 to $18. This brought the tuition price per credit hour for part-time students to the same level as that faced by full-time students. Part-time enrollments jumped 50 per cent in the semester following this price change. Of course, part-time enrollments were escalating even without the tuition reduction. But, perhaps half of the rise might be attributed to the price change alone. More recently, the 1984 decline in enrollments at California's community colleges coincided with the imposition of fees and cutbacks in Federal student aid as well as an improving state economy.

The cutback in institutional appropriations probably affects adult enrollments in higher education even when the institutions are not permitted to raise tuitions. First, where the level of state support is fixed, spaces may be rationed among the applicants. The rationing may be achieved through more rigorous admissions standards. Even if institutions recognise alternate admissions documents for adults (see below), the preparation of these application materials will certainly impose added costs for institutions and students. Second, spaces may be rationed on a "first-come, first-served" basis, rather than on a rolling, continuous admission process. Earlier application deadlines disadvantage adults who often are unaccustomed to academic calenders and unable to anticipate the feasibility of enrolling greatly in advance of the beginning of classes.

Finally, when institutions face falling state appropriations, administrators also look for ways to trim expenditures while sustaining enrollments. An option is to eliminate more expensive, less popular programmes. In 1982, California's community colleges faced a limit on the number of students eligible for state subsidy support. As a result, the institutions were effectively forced to determine how to allocate subsidised enrollments among programmes: should the subsidies sustain and expand the popular non-collegiate vocational/professional programmes or be used to maintain the degree-credit, two-year transfer programmes (CPEC 1982)? Importantly, to the extent degree-credit programmes at community colleges are curtailed, some potential adult students in California might lose their only convenient access to higher education.

2. *Student Financial Support*

The federal government provides most of its support for higher education enrollments through student assistance programmes. Some states, including New York and California, also allocate sizeable amounts of student aid. Yet, although more than a quarter of the enrollments in higher education come from adult populations, relatively small shares of older students actually use student aid to finance their educational expenses. According to data supplied by colleges and universities, some 16 percent of all 1983-84 aid recipients are 26 years of age or older (Stampen 1985; American Council on Education 1984).

Four important sources of student financial support are examined below: grants, entitlements, loans, and private donor aid.

a)   Grants

In the United States, over 2.5 million students each year receive cash grants or scholarships from federal, state, or institutional sources. Most of the available aid dollars are allocated according to financial need, defined as the costs of attendance (tuition and fees, books and supplies, room and board and miscellaneous expenses) *less* a calculated contribution expected from resources available to the student. In 1983-84, the federal Pell grant and SEOG grant programmes provided $3.1 billion, state scholarship and grant programmes (including federal matching funds) accounted for an additional $1.2 billion, and institutions of higher education allocated $2.5 billion from their own, available resources (Gillespie and Carlson 1983). While the programs are not specifically intended to exclude adults, less than one-fifth of the total volume of *federal* grant dollars allocated to undergraduates reached students 25 years of age and older. Less than 15 percent of *all* available grant dollars for undergraduates are received by adult students (estimated from American Council on Education 1984; National Institute of Independent Colleges and Universities 1985). In this case, the provision of grant assistance to students has not promoted adult enrollments because relatively few adults receive sizable, if any, grant or scholarship awards.

The current situation is revealed in Table 9. In the large federal Pell grant programme, some 18 percent of recipients are adults aged 26 and over. This compares to their 26 percent share of total first-degree enrollments. In state scholarship and grant programmes (with a 9 percent share), the Supplemental Educational Opportunity Grant programme (10 percent share), and institutionally-administered grants from other sources (16 percent share), adults in higher education programmes participate in even smaller proportions.

The principal reason for the low representation of adults in grant programmes is a limitation on aid to students engaged in part-time study, the form of attendance most favoured by older students. In the Pell grant programme, which provides cash directly to needy students wherever they live or attend school, only students enrolled half-time or more may receive awards from the programme. Grant aid allocated by institutions, including the federal SEOG dollars, very seldom go to part-time students (and, therefore, to adults). In 1982-83, only 541 students enrolled less-than-half-time received grants through the SEOG programme, a number constituting .08 percent of the programme's recipients (Miller 1985).

Grant and scholarship aid provided through state student assistance programmes have typically excluded part-time students altogether. In 1984-85, 98 percent of all need-based state grant programme recipients were full-time students. But, even this low percent represents an improvement over earlier years. Twenty-three states have recently moved to provide grants to part-timers (NASSGP 1985). Vermont's extension of eligibility for state awards to part-time students directly benefitted adults. Part-time recipients tend to be older (30 years old, on average, in Vermont). Forty per cent are single parents, and 80 per cent of all part-time grant recipients *prefer* to study part-time (Anderson and Meyer 1982).

Of those adults who meet the attendance requirements, many obtain relatively small amounts of grant aid because the need analysis calculations require them to make large contributions and provide unrealistic, inadequate expense allowances (Bowman and Van Dusen 1978; Wagner and Carlson 1983). As just noted, adults usually are treated as independent students, and face expected contribution *rates* and *exemptions* quite similar to those of younger independent students. The problem is that adults stand at a different stage in the life cycle and confront quite different financial demands than these other groups. Thus, the calculations extract larger contributions than can reasonably be expected from adults, making some financially ineligible for grants while preventing others from attending altogether (Wagner 1983b).

Table 9
THE DISTRIBUTION OF STUDENT FINANCIAL AID RECIPIENTS
BY SOURCE AND AGE: 1983-84

	Total	Percentage Distribution Less than 26 Years	26 Years and Over
Total Enrollments	100%	74%	26%
Total Aid Recipients	100	84	16
Pell Grants	100	82	18
Supplemental Grants (SEOG)	100	90	10
State Need-Based Grant	100	91	9
Institution Need-Based Grant	100	84	16
College Work-Study	100	86	14
National Direct Student Loan	100	86	14
Guaranteed Student Loan	100	83	17

Note: The data come from a compilation of financial aid recipient records at a sample of institutions in 1984. Since some aid is allocated and administered outside the institution, not all aid (or recipients) is reflected in the data. Important sources of support for adults which may be under-represented in the data, by as much as 20 percent, include tuition aid and guaranteed student loans.

Source: Estimated from American Council on Education, "Who Gets Student Aid? A 1983-84 Snapshot," 1984; National Institute of Independent Colleges and Universities, "Student Aid Recipient Data Bank, 1983-84," unpublished tabulations, 1985; Stampen, *Student Aid and Public Higher Education Recent Changes*, 1985.

Finally, in making financial aid awards from funds available to the institution, internal policies call for larger "self-help" (loan, work) expectations from, and lower grant awards to, older students. In New York state, Purga (1979) reports that about one-fourth of the institutions package aid differently for adults.

The result of these policies and practices is that adults are not only less likely to receive aid than their younger peers in college, but they also receive smaller average amounts from most of the grant and scholarship programmes. In 1983-84, for example, adult aid recipients received 30 percent smaller total grant amounts than the overall average.

b. Entitlements

Entitlements are vouchers, or chits, that can be applied by the bearer toward post-secondary education expenses. They have the advantage of permitting individuals to schedule higher education whenever it seems most appropriate and beneficial to do so. Presumably, an expansion of entitlements would encourage adults to participate in higher education.

The experience with entitlements in the United States is quite limited. The GI Bill, providing benefits to armed forces veterans, offers the most relevant evidence. The benefits, scaled for family size and attendance status, could be used for up to nine years following discharge from military service. Although eligible programmes ranged to on-the-job and cooperative training, three-fourths of GI Bill recipients in the 1970s chose higher education programmes. Since enrollments occured after service commitments had been met, the beneficiaries tended to be older than the traditional college age group. In 1980, an estimated 70 per cent were over 25 years of age. And nearly two-thirds of those elgible to use the benefits actually did so. This can be compared to a 40 to 50 per cent enrollment rate among non-veterans (see Levin 1979; CBO 1982). However, the educational benefits programme which replaced the GI Bill in 1977 will yield a 15 per cent participation rate when fully phased in. The new programme differs from the old GI Bill in two key ways: 1) it requires contributions while the prospective student is still in the armed services; and 2) the benefit levels are considerably lower. It may be that the success of the GI Bill in generating adult enrollments in higher education resulted as much from the size of the benefits as from the structure and delivery of the subsidy.

The Pell Grant and Guaranteed Student Loan (GSL) programmes offer some additional evidence on the effects of entitlements. Pell grants can be used for educational expenses wherever the student attends college. Although a source of funds which must be repaid, the GSL can similarly be used by a qualifying student enrolled in any eligible programme of study. Both Pell and GSL provide aid "directly" to students, in that students are directly informed about their eligibility for assistance. They differ from GI Bill benefits in their amounts and elibility requirements (limited to needy students enrolled in a narrower range of post-secondary education programmes).

Although the participation rate among "potential" adult students eligible for the grants and loans is very difficult to estimate, it is likely to be lower than that experienced in the GI Bill programme. Nonetheless, in comparison with other student aid programmes, the Pell grant and GSL programmes have been relatively more advantageous to adults. As shown in Table 9, about 18 per cent of Pell grant recipients are at least 26 years old. In the GSL programme, adults account for 17 percent of the recipients. About one-sixth of higher education enrollees 26 years of age or older receive Pells; the comparable proportion for GSL's is slightly more than one-tenth. When the need analysis and attendance criteria which determine eligibility for the grants are considered, the shares of eligible adults participating in the programmes are certainly significant. Still, the existing criteria tend to limit the effectiveness of the programmes in promoting adult participation in higher education.

c. Loans

Two federal student loan programs, Guaranteed Student Loans (GSL) and National Direct Student Loans (NDSL), provide access to credit for low and middle income students enrolled in higher education courses. Through the GSL programme, the federal government establishes a fixed, competitive, guaranteed yield to private lenders originating the loans, and below market interest rates to students (the difference between the current market rate and the student loan rate is met by the federal government). In the NDSL programme, the federal government provides funds to institutions of higher education for lending. Within certain guidelines, the individual colleges and universities establish criteria for allocating the loan funds to needy students and for servicing the loans.

Adults in higher education are using funds provided through these programmes. From Table 9, an estimated 17 per cent of 1983-84 GSL recipients and 14 percent of NDSL recipients were 26 years of age or older. Federal loans, alone, accounted for an estimated 40% of the total amount of aid and provided an average $1500 for these adult recipients in 1983-84 (estimated from American Council on Education 1984; National Institute of Independent Colleges and Universities 1985). These figures are surprising, given the factors working against the use of loan financing by adults. Many adults already have accumulated sizeable debts for homes, autos, and consumer durables. Moreover, in purely economic terms, the adult borrower has fewer years to privately "pay off" on his/her investment in higher education.

Why, then, have adults made such extensive use of student loans? First, loan financing represents one of the few sources of non-family funds available to them. As noted above, adults are less likely to receive grant funds. Second, procedures for acquiring a GSL, and other programme provisions, make this source more readily available. In particular, students acquire GSL financing through banks; if they meet the eligibility criteria, institutions simply will administer the loan proceeds. Third, the below-market interest rate and other implicit subsidy features make federal loans a very attractive financing source.

To the extent federal loan programmes (particularly GSL) remain accessible to adults, they are likely to continue as a major source of external financing for adults in higher education. However, recent changes in the GSL programme call for a more restrictive needs test and a tighter administration of application and disbursement procedures. The latter changes impose more cumbersome procedures which may reduce adult participation in the programme.

Several other novel proposals would expand available financing through employer administered "educational savings plans" or the development of small revolving educational loan funds in community organisations. Clearly, the employer-sponsored or "self-financed" educational savings plans tend to benefit the employed and/or adults with higher tax liabilities, i.e. the "advantaged." As yet, the experience with these new loan forms has been limited (Hauptman 1982).

d. Private Sources

Private external sources of support for degree-credit higher education, such as employer tuition-aid or education leave programmes, have not been widely used in the United States. Although adults would stand to benefit from these programs, perhaps 5 percent of eligible employees actually participate (American Society for Training and Development 1985a). Beyond simply a lack of employee interest, some argue that restrictions on the use of eligible programmes and the provision of funds discourage their use (Smith 1982; Stacey and Charner 1982; O'Neil 1981).

Not surprisingly, tuition aid programmes generally support the development of job-related skills. Information culled from a 1984 survey of employers implies that the programs primarily support enrollments in colleges or universities. Although precise estimates are not presented in the survey report, the survey responses suggest that perhaps two-fifths of employees receiving tuition aid enroll in degree-credit courses. Other employees participate in programs ranging from remedial to vocational/technical to graduate-level study (ASTD 1985a).

Whatever the experience in the past, the use of private sources of support — to students and institutions of higher education — might well increase into the 1990s. Gladieux (1983) anticipates little potential for growth in public student assistance or institutional subsidies. Students and institutions will increasingly turn to the private sector as a source of student aid funds. Beyond support provided by employers and other sources outside colleges or universities, however, adults appear to receive relatively few of these private dollars. Adults are not only less likely to receive student aid grants from institutional funds generated from private contributions, endowment income, and tuition income, they also tend to obtain roughly one-third smaller institutional grant awards than traditional college-age recipients (estimated from National Institute of Independent Colleges and Universities 1985; Table 9).

Others point to potentially greater developed "tastes" for higher education from a more highly educated population. In this case, adults may decide to take up higher education courses with their own funds or look to employers to finance the enrollments. Employers might well accommodate these "consumption" demands for education, if they are unable to offer the promotions, raises, and "meaningful" jobs available to workers in previous generations (Carnevale 1983). Again, those adults already advantaged appear to be most able to tap the private sources of support. However, if programmes for adults expand as a result, all adults — including the disadvantaged — might be able to benefit via reduced per student costs (through scale economies and differential tuitions which take into account only the marginal costs of added enrollments).

3. Tax Expenditures

Adult participation in higher education has been partially supported through tax policies which permit deductions or exemptions for specified education-related activities. These deductions or exemptions involve implicit subsidies in the form of reduced taxes for institutions, students, employers, and donors. In 1980, federal tax expenditures for higher education activities amounted to an estimated $2.8 billion, with less than a third of the total benefitting adults. State tax expenditures in the same year totaled $4.3 billion, with a like proportion supporting adults in higher education (5). There are several tax provisions which appear to benefit adults.

First, scholarship and GI Bill benefits are excluded from income subject to tax. For participating veterans, this provision will save them an estimated $150 million in unassessed taxes in 1983.

Second, employer tuition aid is excluded from income subject to tax. The Office of Management and Budget places the tax benefit to participants at $55 million in 1983. As noted above, these programmes continue to have low participation rates among eligible employees (Smith 1982; ASTD 1985a). The tax treatment of the benefit apparently has not greatly affected its expansion or use. The tax provision excluding tuition aid from taxable income has recently been renewed, but the U.S. Congress may not be inclined to permanently retain it.

Third, all workers can deduct educational expenses necessary to maintain employment in their occupations. While no independent estimate of the value of these tax savings to participants in degree-credit programmes is available, the amount is likely to be relatively small compared to their use in non-credit or post-graduate professional education courses.

Finally, recent changes in the tax code extend the child care tax *credit* to a spouse who is a student. The credit, a dollar-for-dollar offset against taxes owed, is limited to 20 per cent of related child care expenses (up to $2 000). Again, no estimates of the value or effects of this provision are available.

B. ADMISSIONS AND CREDITING

Among the policy and programme changes most directed toward adults are those in admissions and crediting procedures (Squires 1978). By comparison, admission and credit policies at United States higher education institutions have been more flexible and open than in European systems. However, changes

101

over over the 1970s have ushered in procedures even more responsive to the special circumstances of adults.

In a major 1978 survey of institutions, admissions officers reported a continuing use of the high school degree or its equivalent, and achievement test scores in admissions decisions (6). What is noteworthy in the survey responses, shown in Table 10, is the large share of institutions willing to waive requirements for adults. While 88 per cent of all institutions required high school graduation, 30 per cent would waive the requirement for adults. Seventy per cent required admissions test scores, but, at over half of the institutions, adults were not required to submit scores. Public two-year institutions were, at once, least likely to require credentials and most likely to make exceptions for adults.

Table 10
ADMISSIONS PRACTICES IN INSTITUTIONS OF HIGHER EDUCATION: 1978-79

Credential	Percent of Institutions Requiring of All or Some Applicants:				
	All Institutions	Public Four—Year	Public Two—Year	Private Four—Year	Private Two—Year
Evidence of high school graduation or GED	88%	95%	81%	89%	93%
waived for adults or not required	30%	21%	48%	24%	15%
Admissions test scores such as ACT or SAT	70%	90%	32%	84%	64%
waived for adults or not required	55%	38%	76%	50%	57%
Portfolio, statement, audition to document prior work	23%	28%	16%	26%	19%
Letters of recommendation	39%	24%	17%	60%	49%
Interviews with admissions staff, faculty	32%	29%	37%	30%	40%
Personal essay or statement	25%	17%	9%	40%	15%
EXCEPTIONS FOR ADULTS					
Adults as share of exceptions granted	10%	12%	45%	12%	25%

Source: American Association of Collegiate Registrars and Admissions Officers (AAC-RAO) and the College Board, *Undergraduate Admissions*, 1980, Tables 31, 42, and 44.

While aptitude tests declined in use through 1978, the officials at the institutions surveyed expected a rise in their use to 1985 (AACRAO and the College Board 1980). This latter finding, however, partly reflects the wider use of tests as an alternate means of awarding credit. Over two-thirds (67 per cent) of the institutions, including large proportions of four-year colleges, granted credit for acceptable performance on nationally administered examinations. A much smaller share, 13 per cent, award credit based on the evaluations of portfolios documenting prior learning. The recognition of prior learning through evaluation of portfolios has been advanced through the extensive programmes of the Council for the Advancement of Experiential Learning (CAEL 1979).

By 1984, however, while facing continued budget pressures and a renewed interest in institutional quality, over a quarter of all institutions were reviewing or had recently completed a review of admissions proceedures for older students. Importantly, almost three-fifths of the two-year colleges engaged in such a review (El-Khawas 1985).

Whether these reviews presage a retreat from more flexible, accomodating admissions and crediting proceedures, have the policies and practices been effective in promoting the participation of adults in higher education? The evidence is just not clear on this point. Certainly, the large numbers of adults enrolled at two-year colleges can be attributed, in part, to a more open admissions policy. However, these institutions also tend to provide classes at low cost, at convenient times, and at locations near to the work sites or homes of participants (the latter non-traditional attendance options are discussed below). With respect to the awarding of credit through examination, the available data are contradictory. As reviewed in Wagner (1978a), most reports of "induced" enrollments rely on weak, anecdotal evidence. Data from the College Board's College-Level Examination Programme seem to indicate that test-takers are within the traditional college-age groups *and* enrolled full-time when they sat for the exams. The extent to which admissions and/or crediting policies at traditional higher education institutions have stimulated adult enrollments, then, remains unknown.

C. NON-TRADITIONAL ATTENDANCE OPTIONS

Non-traditional attendance options, such as evening, weekend, or summer scheduling, correspondence and telecommunications courses (distance study), part-time study, and off-campus class sites, provide a more flexible and convenient delivery of instruction than traditional, day-time, full-time resident programmes. As shown in Table 11, many existing and newly-developed institutions are providing one or more of these options.

First, about three-fifths of the colleges and universities offer degree credit courses during the summer, in the evenings, or on weekends. At the associate degree level, 92 per cent of two-year colleges schedule classes at these times. At the bachelor's degree level, almost all doctoral-level or comprehensive four-year institutions offer classes during the summer. By comparison, evening or weekend programmes are scheduled by over four-fifths (84 per cent) of the doctoral and comprehensive institutions and by slightly less than three-fourths (70 percent) of general baccalaureate colleges. Interestingly, 16 percent of all

103

colleges and universities — and more than a quarter of the doctoral and comprehensive institutions — offer a weekend college program. In recent years, the number of institutions offering degree-credit courses at convenient times has grown. However, much of the increase in these non-traditional programmes has resulted from the addition of newly recognized institutions of higher education rather than the development of non-traditional programmes at existing institutions.

Second, somewhat smaller numbers of institutions offer degree-credit instruction away from the main campus. In 1972-73, one-fifth of the institutions offered classes in community centers, local schools, churches, libraries, museums, or at work sites. Although the share seems relatively small, one should keep in mind that most communities already have a two-year college within a short drive for most residents. And, by 1985, fueled by adult demands and public policy pressure, the share of institutions offering degree-credit classes off-campus has certainly increased. In Kansas, for example, a revision in the state funding formulae to include off-campus FTE in the enrollment base was accompanied by a one-third increase in off-campus FTE generated by the Board of Regents institutions. Public officials in Indiana have taken a different

Table 11
INSTITUTIONS OF HIGHER EDUCATION OFFERING
NON-TRADITIONAL ATTENDANCE OPTIONS: 1983-84

Option	Percent of Institutions Offering:			
	All Institutions	Doctoral, Comprehensive Four-Year	General Baccalaureate	Two-Year
Summer Session(1)				
Associate Degree	59%	45%	44%	92%
Bachelor's Degree	59%	96%	85%	38%
Evening/Weekend(1)				
Associate Degree	55%	42%	38%	92%
Bachelor's Degree	54%	84%	70%	42%
Weekend				
College Program	16%	26%	16%	11%
External				
Degree Program	19%	29%	14%	17%
Correspondence	10%			
Part-Time Study (2)				
To meet all of				
degree requirements	68%			
Off-Campus sites (2)	21%			

1. All institution percents include specialized and new institutions, which are not shown separately.
2. Based on responses to items in 1972 survey of institutions.
Source: U.S. Department of Education, National Center for Education Statistics, *Education Directory 1983–84*, 1985b, Table 8; El-Khawas, *Campus Trends 1984*, 1985, Table 1; Cross and Valley, *Planning Non-Traditional Programs*, 1974.

approach. Rather than establishing a regional campus in the under-served Elkhart area, the Indiana Commission for Higher Education has explored the possibilities for providing post-high school educational opportunities through a collaboration among existing community groups, local employers, and local and state institutions and agencies. As one state official describet it:

> The metaphor we have chosen to help illustrate the differences between the Elkhart project and a regional campus is that the Elkhart project is being thought of as a shopping center of stores, as opposed to a full-service department store owned by one company (Scott 1982).

Under the Elkhart proposal, local organisations and employers would provide administrative oversight, instructional sites, and some financing. Instruction would be provided by local schools as well as by colleges and universities from other parts of the state. The most intriguing aspect of the proposal is that particular academic or vocational programs would be provided by a college or university best equipped to deliver it (e.g., general academic programs at the undergraduate level by a liberal arts college; business, health, and science programs by Indiana University; engineering and technology programs by Purdue University).

Finally, although barely 10 per cent of colleges and universities have sizeable home study, or correspondence, programmes, these seem to be growing (if in different forms). Most of the existing programmes are operated through the extension divisions of large universities, but departments or schools within institutions often conduct their own programmes.

Have the non-traditional attendance options encouraged adult enrollments in higher education? Information from a variety of sources suggests the answer is yes. Large numbers of adults enroll in evening and correspondence classes, providing some casual evidence of the effects of the scheduling and location of classes. More detailed analytical studies continue to show the sizeable independent effects of distance to class site on the enrollment of adults (Bishop and Van Dyke 1977; Froomkin and Wolfson 1977). Some evidence from California seems to indicate that minority populations find the "off-campus" sites more familiar and less threatening (i.e., more accessible) than college classrooms. In sum, policies leading to the offering of instruction at more convenient times and places do promote the participation of adults in higher education.

D. NEW INSTITUTIONS AND PROVIDERS

Finally, new institutions have been established which offer a quite different approach than the alternatives available through the traditional institutions of higher education. These new colleges include distance study collegiate institutions, "certification" institutions, and colleges offering "learner contract" arrangements.

Several distance study, TV colleges continue to provide higher education courses to a large number of students. One of the more ambitious distance study efforts was undertaken by the University of Mid-America, in Omaha. However, UMA no longer exists. Beyond the general problem of establishing a new institution during a period of tight budgets and a relatively weak economy, the University of Mid-America failed for a number of reasons: (1) they worked through a consortia of existing institutions in the region who had little incentive to promote the use of the TV courses; (2) the courses did not respond to the demands of UMA's market. The subscriptions might have been greater for a personal investment course, rather than a course on China or beginning psychology; and (3) UMA developed very polished and costly TV courses. Thus, rather than an extensive listing of adequate TV courses, it appears UMA opted for a smaller number of high quality offerings.

The picture is a bit different for "certification" institutions. These are institutions established primarily to *certify* college-level competencies (e.g., the Regents' College Degree programme in New York State, Edison College in New Jersey). Enrollees do not participate in courses of the institution; rather they submit transcripts, achievement test scores, and other documentation to the institution for evaluation. Those who can establish the adequacy of their college-level skills are awarded degrees.

The "certification" institutions as well as extensive certification programs in existing institutions have generally been successful. The Regents' College Degree program, for example, currently has 16,000 actively seeking degrees. Students pay an enrollment fee of $175. For each year they remain in the program, students pay a records maintenance fee of $100 (associate level) or $150 (baccalaureate level). Students also bear the costs for written examinations which afford credit ($30 to $225 each) and oral examinations ($350). In 1985, over 3,000 degrees were awarded.

Finally, a number of "learner contract" institutions have been established apart from (and more recently within) existing colleges and universities. The essential feature of these institutions is that students set up their own programme of study (a "learner contract"), subject to the approval of the faculty advisor. Credit can be earned through regular course attendance, at any college or university, or through the evaluation of work experience or knowledge. In 1984, about one-fifth of all institutions offered the external degree study option (Table 11). Some programmes are quite diverse and far-ranging (Empire State College in New York, University Without Walls), while some are very focussed on certain fields, locales, and needs (California State University Consortium, Kansas University programme). All programmes, however, emphasize some link to a college campus and/or staff member as a vital key to ensure quality and to gain acceptance for the degree.

These programs apparently serve an older, employed population of potential students. Survey information obtained from a small number of Empire State College students in one area of New York State indicate that the typical student was likely to be older than 40, female, and employed in professional or technical occupations. Sizable proportions, however, were employed in clerical occupations or not working. Over half the students financed the costs of attendance out of their own earnings or their spouse's income. Federal and state grants as well as support from employers were used by more than a quarter of the survey respondents (Empire State College 1985).

The staying-power of these innovations is unknown. First, while the placement experience and employer acceptance has been good, the evidence to date reflects the experiences of a self-selected group. Some findings on the marketability of the external or learner contract degrees heavily reflect their use by civil service and education professionals who must meet rigid education requirements for promotions or salary raises in their fields, or by those currently employed. It is not clear whether the same results would obtain, for example, for adults wishing to change occupations in the private sector. Second, with some exceptions, the programmes do not receive the same level of public subsidy support as do traditional college and university programmes. In California, the CSU Consortium must meet the full costs of its programme through student fees. Without substantial state support, the programme recruits teachers and advisors on a part-time, added assignment basis.

On the other hand, existing colleges and universities have been willing to adopt several of the innovations introduced by the free-standing new institutions. Both the California Consortium and the Kansas University programme clearly operate within the existing university structure. Similar expansions in television courses (Kansas) have also occurred. But, even where these new approaches are adopted, college and university programmes tend to be more restrictive and less innovative than programmes in the free-standing institutions. The danger is that increasing competition for the pool of external and learner contract degree students will more severely affect the more flexible free-standing institutions. And, if the latter institutions are unable to offer the full array of programs or services (or are unable to survive), the availability of truly flexible non-traditional external and learner contract degree opportunities for adults may be more limited.

E. STUDENT SUPPORT SERVICES

The special circumstances of adults often require services of a different type and at different times than is true for students of traditional age. However, relatively few institutions provide these services. In 1972-73, about one-tenth provided child care, although a larger number offered to help students locate these services. By 1984, almost 40 per cent provided day care. However, most programmes are limited to daytime hours. Many close on school holidays and vacations and at night. In general, they cater to college personnel; adults attending night courses are less likely to find day care services available (Kraft 1984).

According to responses to the 1972-73 institutional survey, about half of the

107

institutions provided counselling services before or after evening or weekend classtimes. Library facilities and study areas were commonly kept open (by an estimated 82 per cent of the colleges), but laboratories were less commonly available for use. At about half of the institutions (58 per cent), bookstore and cafeteria services continued into evening and weekend hours (Cross and Valley 1974). These figures refer to the availability of student support services over ten years ago; the situation has likely improved since then (7).

However, the accumulated evidence on the provision of these services reveals nothing about their effects on the enrollment choices of adults. Without doubt, student support services facilitate enrollments. But, adults may find the availability of these services at the institution less limiting than financial, admissions, scheduling, and attendance policies.

Chapter III
Further continuing education

In 1983-84, an estimated 6 million students participated in non-credit or credit-bearing courses as non-degree students in U.S. colleges and universities (Table 7). Of these, perhaps one million attended undergraduate degree-credit courses (estimated from U.S. Department of Education 1985c). Although large, these numbers do not reflect significant increases over the early 1980's. The relatively slow growth in college and university-based continuing education can be partly explained by programmes and practices of institutions and the implicit policies of public agencies.

A. FINANCING

Further education at colleges and universities is financed through public appropriations to institutions, direct support to participants from public and private sources, contracts with employers and private firms, indirect tax subsidies for institutions, participants, and private donors, and the participants' own resources.

1. *Public Institutional Financial Support*
Most states and institutions require further education programmes to be supported entirely through non-institutional sources. This financial test is not applied to any other instructional activity within institutions of higher education. Howard Bowen (1980) points out that, as implemented, the financial test often leads to an inconsistent evaluation of the programmes' costs and revenues. The programmes are asked to be "self-supporting," which usually means generating revenue sufficient to meet the fully-allocated costs of their courses (direct costs plus a "share" of fixed and other support services costs, such as buildings, equipment, and the president's office). At the same time, the programmes are often viewed as incremental to the central instructional mission of the institution. If so, the programmes should be expected to meet only

the added direct and support costs of offering the course (with no, or little, cost reimbursement required for the physical plant or the president's office) (8).

Few states are willing to support non-credit continuing education activities to any significant extent. Kansas' legislature remains to be convinced of the "value" of non-credit education, although state officials report an interest in sustaining specific, job-related non-credit courses. California, one of the most generous states in its support of education, has tightened the criteria governing a course's eligibility for state support. Alternatively, Michigan and Texas remain more generous in their treatment of non-credit enrollments in state budgeting formulas. Still, the general indication is that the "self-support" financial requirement will continue and may increase in importance for all continuing education offerings. The implication is that institutions will be unable to use public institutional subsidies to expand non-credit continuing education programmes, even if they serve to enhance employment prospects and subsequent job performance of adults.

Yet, even without state support, some continuing education courses do pay, and handsomely, for institutions of higher education. In a detailed study of costs and revenues in courses offered through continuing education units, part-time courses which could be creditable (eg. typing and accounting) were found to "make money" for the institution (Anderson and Kasl 1981). The program-mes report a revenue of about $5 per student contact hour, while spending $2.50 to $3.00 per hour on the courses. Few of the less rigorous non-credit courses generate a surplus, but this conclusion is based on a comparison of revenues with fully-allocated average costs (Wagner 1984).There appears to be a need for a re-assessment of state and institutional policies governing the evaluation of the costs of and resources for continuing education. In the meantime, adults will have to draw on other public and private sources of funds to cover course expenses.

2. Student Financial Support

Adults undertaking continuing education face an either/or situation. Those participating in employer-sponsored programmes at universities and colleges typically pay none of the out-of-pocket costs of the course. Others must meet expenses from their own resources, with some help from public tax expenditure benefits and various sources of credit.

Employers have become an increasingly important source of financial support for adults in college and university continuing education programmes. Employers currently provide support for about two-fifths of college and univer-sity courses attended by part-timers. This proportion is up substantially from 1978 (estimated from U.S. Department of Education 1985d). However, it is important to note that colleges and universities still attract a relatively small share of employer support for continuing education and training. Overall, about a quarter of all courses supported by employers are provided by institu-tions of higher education (estimated from U.S. Department of Education

110

1985d). Within the banking industry, some 6 percent of the training volume was provided through educational institutions (American Society for Training and Development 1985b).

3. Tax Expenditures

As with degree-credit students, participants in job-related continuing education may qualify for a tax deduction in the amount of the course expenses. Given the number of professional education requirements imposed in a number of fields by federal and state governments, the use of this benefit will surely increase (Peterson 1983). Even so, the tax provisions tend to benefit the employed and higher income groups the most. In fact, those undertaking training to *change* careers are specifically excluded.

B. NEW PROVIDERS

In the United States, a growing variety of providers offer avocational-personal interest and development courses. When combined, the tutors, community groups, Agricultural Extension programmes, museums and libraries, local school districts, and colleges and universities annually offer courses attended by at least 22 million, largely adult, participants (updated from Wagner 1983b).

Most innovative among this group are the so-called "Free Universities" and their offshoots. The Free Universities serve as brokering agents between those who want to learn and those willing to teach. About 200 of these programs were identified in 1981 (Table 12). The courses are not free. Participants pay a modest registration fee ($2) and a variable course fee (depends on the number of class hours and necessary supplies). Indeed, 90 per cent of the revenues of Free University-type institutions come from participant fees (Table 12). Some of the courses are clearly at a first-degree level (personal finance, basic computer skills, some arts courses).

One of the most interesting free universities is the University for Man, in Manhattan, Kansas. UFM has been particularly successful in developing rural community-based education programmes. Within 20 or 30 communities throughout the state, a local programme director (usually just an interested resident) co-ordinates the schedule of classes. UFM has experimented in other states with using Cooperative Extension agents and librarians as programme directors. The UFM staff believe their success in these small rural towns comes from (1) local involvement in programme planning and development and (2) the personal contact afforded in the classes. Instruction via telecommunications provides neither of these features.

At the other extreme, employers and private training firms have greatly expanded their own efforts in job-related training. Among the more recent trends: (1) the volume of training in industry has been increasing at a rate of 20 per cent per year; (2) commercial training firm volume has grown at twice the rate of growth of industry training; and, (3) the commercial training sector is dominated by a few large firms, but small, typically one-person firms are in the majority. In part, the growth of the private training firms has helped to meet a rapidly escalating demand from industry for training, and college and university continuing education programmes have also contributed to meeting this demand. However, many of the one-person training firms are, in fact, college and university faculty members accepting "outside" part-time employment. In effect, we have a situation where continuing education programme staff compete with their own faculty colleagues in providing employer training programs.

Table 12

PROGRAMMES AND FINANCES OF FREE UNIVERSITIES: 1981

	Total	Percent	College Related Total	Percent	Other Total	Percent
Registrations (000's)	547		259		288	
Institutions	187		111		76	
Populations eligible to participate						
Open to all	145	77.5	74	66.7	71	93.4
Adults only	8	4.3	7	6.3	1	1.3
College-related	27	14.4	27	24.3	-	-
Other	7	3.7	3	2.7	4	5.3
Programs offered						
Classes	183	97.9	111	100.0	72	94.7
Referrals	20	10.7	11	9.9	9	11.8
Cooperative	29	15.5	12	10.8	17	22.4
Other	20	10.7%	7	6.3	13	17.1
Income by Source						
Total Revenue (000's)	$8 389	100.0	$2 666	100.0	$5 /723	100.0
Institutional support	378	45.0	353	13.2	25	.4
Fees	7 541	90.0	2 /128	79.8	5 413	94.6
Contracts/grants	175	2.1	149	5.6	26	.4
Other	294	3.5	128	4.8	166	2.9

Source: Litkowksi, "Free Universities and Learning Referral Centers, 1981,"
NCES Report 83-312, 1983a.

Adults certainly participate in avocational and job-related continuing education within and outside of colleges and universities. More recently, the continuing education programmes of higher education institutions have moved to emulate some of the more successful innovations of the non-university providers. Many colleges have incorporated avocational "free university" offerings within their continuing education programme. By the early 1980s, about two-thirds of the free universities were, in fact, affiliated with an institution of higher education (Table 12). Techniques for marketing, scheduling, and pricing of courses have been adopted, as well. These changes have facilitated adult participation in avocational non-credit courses at institutions of higher education.

Similarly, institutions of higher education have attempted to exploit their unique advantages in job-related continuing education programming. As shown in Table 13, about half of all colleges and universities now provide credit and non-credit courses at the job site. This proportion has increased by about 50% since 1981. Other initiatives, such as developing joint degree programs or sharing instructors, are less common, but they do reflect a growing range of collaborative educational ventures between higher education and the private sector.

The reasons for the growing collaboration seem obvious. First, as firms confront sizeable expenses in mounting their own training efforts, college-based continuing education programmes offer a cost-effective alternative. Through special financing incentives, states have further encouraged campus-business linkages. Second, colleges and universities have marshalled resources and attempted to establish programs in ways that accomodate the needs of employers. Some institutions have established institutes to provide training and assistance to employers in particular industries. Since the institutes independently employ staff to meet training needs, they also have been used to retain the faculty members who might otherwise provide industry training on a private, consulting basis.

More important are the initiatives for adults who might not receive inexpensive, continuing education from other providers. Small businesses and individuals wishing to acquire new or advanced skills represent two such adult clientele groups.

Table 13
COLLEGE AND UNIVERSITY TIES WITH BUSINESS AND INDUSTRY: 1984

Option	Percent of Institutions Offering:			
	All Institutions	Doctoral, Comprehensive Four-Year	General Baccalaureate	Two-Year
Credit courses for business employees at business locations	47.3%	48.8%	25.5%	58.9%
Non-credit courses for business employees at business locations	48.2	49.7	27.2	59.3
Jointly developed and sponsored degree programs	19.3	17.4	9.3	25.8
Shared or on-loan staff	18.8	28.2	15.8	16.4

Source: El-Khawas, Campus Trends 1984, 1985, Table 8.

Conclusions

A. INSTITUTIONAL RESPONSES TO PRESSURES AND POLICIES

Whether the public commitment to higher education in the United States will wane, adults will increasingly be involved in programmes offered by institutions of higher education. The increase in the numbers of adults, a growing competition in world markets for United States goods and services, and the widening gap between the supplies of and demands for skilled workers all point toward a private and public demand for adult education and training. Colleges and universities will likely provide the higher and further education courses adults may require to improve performance on the job.

It now appears that the responsibiltity and funding for training is shifting to employers. In part, this shift follows on the need for skilled workers, not all of which can be accommodated throught the natural attrition and replacement of less skilled older workers with younger, newly trained job entrants. But, the shift also reflects a growing perception that United States higher education may not be responding quickly enough to the needs of the workplace. This, it would seem, is a break from the past, when colleges were looked to as sources of improvements in technical competence.

A second theme for the 1980s concerns the provision of educational opportunities for those unable to draw upon their own, or their employers's resources. The less educated, displaced workers lack access to employer-provided programmes. Increasing numbers of mature age females, many with dated skills, are joining the workforce. How can colleges and universities meet the needs of these adults?

With these trends as backdrop, this report has reviewed existing patterns in adult participation in higher and further education and considered how selected financial and organisational policies and programmes enable or retard greater adult involvement in the United States. Several broad findings merit emphasis.

B. PUBLIC POLICY IMPACTS

First, adults appear less likely to participate in the full-time, degree-credit programmes, and most likely to choose non-degree, part-time courses, than their younger counterparts. While the part-time courses may better serve the education needs of adults, public subsidies tend to flow to the full-time programmes. This raises a major policy question: should part-time, even non-degree, programmes receive greater public support?

Second, few public financing policies have earmarked their benefits for adults in higher and further education programmes. Only selected tax policies, such as the deductability of appropriate professional education expenses for workers and the exclusion of employee educational benefits from taxable income, provide financial benefits primarily to adults. The development of the community college system, on the other hand, was not intended to promote adult enrollments in higher education, even though the existence of these institutions clearly encouraged many adults to enroll.

Third, small numbers of eligible adults have used the public or private financing options available to them. Entitlement schemes, such as the new GI Bill and the Pell grant programme, show 15 to 20 per cent usage rates among those eligible . Tuition aid, available from employers, is used by 2 to 5 per cent of covered, eligible employees. These financing options share several unattractive features, including restrictions on eligible programmes and uses and a lack of funds to meet the "up-front" tuition and books costs of higher education courses. Importantly, these are particularly difficult burdens for those most in need of the training, such as the unemployed and adult female labour force entrants.

Fourth, whether through inertia, response to incentives and constraints, or conscious policy decisions, institutions appear less likely to allocate unrestricted available dollars to programmes serving adults, or to adult participants. The pressures work against programmes serving adults. On the one hand, institutions face very real incentives to seek out and apply funds to the most profitable, remunerative programme. The danger is that some of the smaller programmes may provide unique opportunities for adults (e.g., degree-credit courses in community colleges). At the same time, the encouragement to seek out industry linkages (and financial support) raises the risk that the privately-directed training demands may not fully reflect longer term public interests which institutions of higher education have traditionally served. The questions here go to concerns about the role of institutions of higher education in providing opportunities for adults.

Finally, some initiatives have been quite successful. Free-standing, external degree institutions, free universities, and commercial training ventures have all successfully provided higher and further education opportunities for adults. And, it is clear that colleges and universities have adopted the innovations in some way. The admissions and crediting practices have become more flexible at all institutions of higher education, with credit-by-exam, portfolio evaluations, and "learner contract" arrangements. Distance teaching, new telecommunications technologies, and free university-type programmes have all been expanded and improved within traditional colleges and universities. College-based training institutes have successfully entered a growing job-related training market.

What is not clear is whether these changes have greatly increased adult enrollments in institutions of higher education. Programmes providing "credit" for prior learning tend to draw heavily from younger age groups. Novel instructional formats offering flexible, student-designed programmes of study have met with mixed success. Enrollments remain modest partly because the value of the degree has just not been widely demonstrated to employers or adults. Although increasing, adult participation in non-credit avocational or job-related further education at colleges and universities grows more slowly than in programmes of non-school providers.

The existing policies and programmes have only partly met the challenge of providing higher and further education opportunities for adults in the 1980s. The expansion of initiatives such as college/industry linkages and non-traditional attendance options hold great promise. But, all will require the kind of timely, effective response from policy makers and institutions that has been lacking in the past.

NOTES

1. These data underestimate the actual volume of non-credit activities, since courses may be offered by departments and schools as well as the extension divisions within institutions of higher education.
2. Adult males are equally likely to benefit. During the 1981-82 recession, unemployment among older male workers increased in line with other population groups. The data continue to show, however, that those with higher education were least affected by the unemployment rise.
3. These patterns mirror those reported in other studies of adults in higher education. See, in particular, Solmon and Gordon (1981).
4. Too, some states weight their funding formulas in such a way that institutions receive less revenue per credit hour for part-time enrollments. The resulting difference between fully-allocated costs and reduced state support is usually met through higher fees.
   Some differential may be justified if part-time students impose higher costs per credit hour, for administrative and support services. However, if the part-time programmes are truly "incremental," then they should be evaluated in terms of the actual added costs imposed. The added costs of putting on additional courses to accommodate part-time learners must be quite modest, given the availability of existing facilities and administrative services already in place. See Brinkman (1985).
5. The estimates come from Brinkman (1982). Parental personal exemptions for dependent students and the exclusion of Social Security student benefits account for two-thirds of the federal tax expenditures for higher education. State local tax expenditures include sales tax exemptions, the deductability of contributions on state and

local income taxes, and property tax exemptions. If these latter tax savings are apportioned by enrollments, perhaps one-third of the sum could be credited to adults.

6. The GED is awarded to those who successfully pass an examination of comptencies expected of high school graduates. The credential is widely recognized as the equivalent of a high school degree.

7. Non-profit organizations, community-based coalitions of private and public sector interest groups, and state agencies also offer information and counseling services for adults. A recent survey of state financial aid agency efforts to disseminate information uncovered programs targetted on adult populations in 19 states (Hauptman and Gruss 1984). The information and services provided to adults varies widely from state to state and among communities within states.

8. There is no "appropriate" way to allocate overhead expenses. These are matters of institutional goals and purposes, subject to negotiation. The central issue is the extent to which further education programmes are peripheral to the institution's mission. If they are, very little overhead should be charged against continuing education activities. See Wagner (1983a).

REFERENCES

American Association of Collegiate Registrars and Admissions Officers (AACRAO) and the College Board. *Undergraduate Admissions*. New York: The College Board, 1980.

American Council on Education. "Who Gets Student Aid: A 1983-84 Snapshot," tabulations. Washington, D.C.: Author, 1984.

American Society for Training and Development. *Employee Educational Assistance*. Washington, D.C.: Author, 1985a.

— *Training Americas Bankers*. Washington, D.C.: Author, 1985b.

Anderson, Britta and Elizabeth Meyer. *Socio-Economic and Educational Characteristics of Vermont Part-Time Grant Program Applicants and Students*. Winooski, VT: Vermont Student Assistance Corporation, 1982.

Anderson, Richard E., and Gordon Darkenwald. *Participation and Persistence in American Adult Education*. New York: The College Board, 1979.

— "The Adult Part-Time Learner in Colleges and Universities: A Clientele Analysis", *Research in Higher Education* 10 (Winter 1979): 357-70.

Anderson, Richard E., and Elizabeth Swain Kasl. *The Costs and Financing of Adult Education and Training*. Lexinton, MA: Lexington Books, 1982.

Arbeiter, Solomon, Carol B. Aslanian, Frances A. Schmerbeck, and Henry M. Brickell. *40 Million Americans in Career Transition The Need for Information*. New York: College Entrance Examination Board, 1978.

Aslanian, Carol B., and Henry M. Brickell. *Americans in Transition Life Changes as Reasons for Adult Learning*. New York: College Entrance Examination Board, 1980.

Association of Colleges and Universities of the State of New York (ACUSNY), "Higher Education in New York State," unpublished manuscript. Albany, NY: Author, 1986.

Astin, Helen. *Some Action of Her Own The Adult Woman and Higher Education*. Lexington, MA: Lexington Books, 1976.

Bishop, John, and Jane Van Dyk. "Can Adults Be Hooked on College? Some Determinants of Adult College Attendance," *Journal of Human Resources* 48 (Spring 1977): 39-62.

Bowen, Howard R. *Adult Learning Higher Education and the Economics of Unused Capacity*. New York: The College Board, 1980.

Bowman, James L., and William D. Van Dusen. *The Determinants of Financial Need for Adults in Post-Secondary Education.* Princeton, NJ: Educational Testing Service, 1978.

Brinkman, Paul. "Higher Eduacation Financing: 1973-1980," *Research Report.* Boulder, CO: NCHEMS, November, 1982.

— "The Financial Impact of Part-Time Enrollments on Two-Year Colleges: A Marginal Cost Perspective," *Journal of Higher Education* 56 (May/June 1985): 338-53.

California Post-Secondary Education Commission. *Implication of Budget Act Language to Reduce State Apportionments to Community College Districts by 30 Million.* Sacramento: Author, 1982a.

— *Learning Activities of California Adults.* Sacramento: Author: 1982b.

— *Uses of Student Fee Revenues in California Public Higher Education.* Sacramento: Author, 1982c.

Calvert, Jr., Robert. *Non-Credit Activities in Institutions of Higher Education for the Year Ending June 30 1980.* Washington, D.C.: National Center for Education Statistics, 1982.

Carnevale, Anthony P. *Human Capital.* Washington, D.C.: ASTD Press, 1983.

Coffey, Janice. "The ECS/California Lifelong Learning Project: A Case Study," unpublished manuscript. Sacramento: California Postsecondary Education Commission, 1982.

Commission on Non-Traditional Study. *Diversity by Design.* San Francisco: Jossey-Bass, 1973.

Congressional Budget Office. *Improving Military Educational Benefits Effects on Costs Recruiting and Retention.* Washington, D.C.: Government Printing Office, 1982.

— *Tax Expenditures Current Issues and Five-Year Budget Projections for Fiscal Years 1983—88.* Washington, D.C.: Government Printing Office, 1982.

Council for the Advancement of Experiential Learning. *Opportunities for Prior Learning Credit An Annotated Directory.* Columbia, MD: Author, 1979.

Cross, K. Patricia, John R. Valley, and Associates. *Planning Non-Traditional Programs An Analysis of the Issues for Postsecondary Education.* San Francisco: Jossey-Bass, 1974.

El-Khawas, Elaine. *Campus Trends 1984.* Washington, D.C.: American Council on Education, 1985.

Empire State College. "Survey of 1982 Entering Students," unpublished tabulations. Saratoga Springs, NY: Office of Research and Evaluation, Empire State College, 1985.

Froomkin, Joseph, and Robert J. Wolfson. *Adult Education 1972 A Reanalysis.* Washington, D.C.: Joseph Froomkin, Inc., May 1977.

Gillespie, Donald A., and Nancy Carlson. *Trends in Student Aid 1963—1983.* Washington, D.C.: The College Board, 1983 (and updates).

Gladieux, Lawrence E. "The Future of Student Financial Aid," in *Student Financial Aid A Handbook for Practitioners and Academic Administrators,* eds. R.H. Fenske and R.P. Huff. San Francisco: Jossey-Bass, 1983.

Hamilton, I. Bruce. *The Third Century Postsecondary Planning for the Non-Traditional Learner.* Princeton, NJ? Educational Testing Service, 1976.

Hauptman, Arthur. *Financing Student Loans The Search for Alternatives in the Face of Federal Contraction.* Washington, D.C.: The College Board, 1982.

Hauptman, Arthur, and Emily Gruss. "State Agency Infrmation Efforts," *Reports and Papers.* Proceedings from the First Annual NASSGP/NCHELP Research Conference. Springfield, IL: Illinois State Scholarship Commission, 1984: 33-60.

Hill, Susan. "Participants in Postsecondary Education," *NCES Special Report* 84-309. Washington, D.C.: U.S. Department of Education, National Center for Education Statistics, 1984.

Kasper, Gene. "Continuing Education Needs and Interests of Kansas Adult Learners," unpublished manuscript. Topeka: Board of Regents, 1980.

Kraft, Barbara S. "Day Care Programs Take Hold on Campuses," *Chronicle at Higher Education*, 15th February 1984.

Levin, Henry M. "Individual Entitlements" in: H. Levin/H.G. Schütze (eds), *Financing Recurrent Education — Strategies for Increasing Employment, Job Opportunities and Productivity*, Beverly Hills: Sage Publications, 1983.

Levine, Marsha. "Corporate Education and Training," unpublished manuscript. Washington, D.C.: National Commission on Student Financial Assistance, 1982.

Litkowski, Thomas. "Free Universities and Learning Referral Centers, 1981," *NCES Report* 83-312. Washington, D.C.: National Center for Education Statistics, 1983a.

— "Non-Collegiate Postsecondary Schools with Occupational Programs, 1982," *NCES Early Release* 83-309. Washington, D.C.: National Center for Education Statistics, May 1983b.

Michelotti, Kopp. "Educational Attainment of Workers, March 1976," *Monthly Labor Review* 100 (March 1977): 62-65.

Miller, Scott E. "Financial Aid for Part-Time Students: An Update," *Reports and Papers*. Proceedings from the Second Annual NASSGP/NCHELP Research Conference. Springfield, IL: Illinois State Scholarship Commission, 1985: 25-34.

National Association of State Scholarship and Grant Programs. 16th Annual Report 1984—85 Survey Year. Harrisburg: Pennsylvania Higher Education Assistance Agency, 1985.

National Institute of Independent Colleges and Universities, "Student Aid Recipient Data Bank, 1983-84," unpublished tabulations. Washington, D.C.: Author, 1985 (and tabulations from earlier years).

Nollen, Stanley. "The Development and Utilization of Human Resources in the Context of Technological Change and Industrial Restructuring: Human Resource Policies in the United States," unpublished manuscript. Washington, D.C.: Georgetown University, 1985.

O'Neil, Joseph P. *College Financial Aid and the Employee Benefit Programs of the Fortune 500 Companies*. Princeton, NJ: Conference University Press, 1981.

Organization for Economic Co-Operation and Development. *Learning Opportunities for Adults*. Vol. IV: Participation in Adult Education. Paris: OECD, 1977.

— "The Costs and Financing of Recurrent Education," Centre for Educational Research and Innovation. Paris: OECD, 1980; revised version in: H.G Schütze/D. Istance, *Recurrent Education Revisited — Modes of Participation avd Financing* Stockholm: Almquist & Wiksell, 1987 (forthcoming).

Peterson, Richard E. "Continuing Education", unpublished manuscript. Paris: Centre for Educational Research and Innovation, OECD, 1983.

Pitchell, Robert J. *Financing Part-Time Students The New Majority in Postsecondary Education*. Washington, D.C.: American Council on Education, 1974.

Purga, Robert, "Financial Aid and the Adult Learner", unpublished manuscript. Albany, N.Y.: Office of Adult Learning Services, State Education Department, 1979.

Rose, Clare, and Cheryl C. Graesser. *Adult Participation in Lifelong Learning Activities in California*. Sacramento: California Postsecondary Education Commission, October 1981.

Rumberger, Russell W. "Job Market for College Graduates: 1960-90," *Journal* of Higher Education 55 (July/August 1984): 433-54.

Scott, Robert A. "Correspondence with Mr. Keith Meade." Indianapolis: Commission for Higher Education, December 1982.

Smith, Gregory. "Employer-Sponsored Programs," in *Financing Recurrent Education*, ed. H. Levin and H.G. Schutze, Beverly Hills, CA: Sage, 1983.

Solmon, Lewis C., and Joanne J. Gordon. *The Characteristics and Needs of Adults in Postsecondary Education*. Lexington, MA: Lexington Books, 1981.

Squires, G. "Admission Policies in Postsecondary Education: New Groups in Post-

Secondary Education." Paris: OECD, 1978.

Stacy, Nevzer, and Ivan Charner. "Unions and Postsecondary Education," in *Financing Recurrent Education*, ed. H. Levin and H.G. Schutze, Beverly Hills, CA: Sage, 1983.

Stampen, Jacob O. *Student Aid and Public Higher Education Recent Changes*. Washington, D.C.: American Association of State Colleges and Universities, 1985.

State of Kansas, Board of Regents. *Continuing Education Study*. Topeka: Author, 1977.

U.S. Department of Commerce, Bureau of the Census. "School Enrollment — Social and Economic Characteristics of Students: October 1981 and 1980," *Current Population Reports*, P-20, No. 400. Washington, D.C.: U.S. Government Printing Office, 1985 (and previous numbers).

U.S. Department of Education, National Center for Education Statistics. *Condition of Education 1985*. Washington, D.C.: U.S. Government Printing Office, 1985a (and earlier years).

— *Education Directory 1983—84*. Washington, D.C.: U.S. Government Printing Office, 1985b (and earlier years).

— *Fall Enrollment in Colleges and Universities 1983. Washington, D.C.*: U.S. Government Printing Office, 1985c (and earlier years).

— *Participation in Adult Education May 1984*, unpublished tabulations.. Washington, D.C.: Author, 1985d (and earlier years).

— *Projections of Education Statistics to 1992—93*. Washington, D.C.: U.S. Government Printing Office, 1985e (and earlier years).

U.S. Department of Labor, Bureau of Labor Statistics. "Educational Attainment of Workers, 1982-83," *Special Labor Force Report*, Bulletin 2191. Washington, D.C.: U.S. Government Printing Office, 1984.

Wagner, Alan P. "The Economic Impact of Credit by Examination Policies and Practices: Identification of the Issues and Implications for Research," in *The Economic Impact of Credit By Examination*, ed. John R. Valley. Princeton: Educational Testing Service, 1978a: 105-50.

— "Financing Learning Opportunities for Adults Through Existing Student Aid Programs," *School Review* 86 (May 1978b): 410-35.

— "The Definition and Measurement of Participation, Costs, and Financing of Post-Compulsory Education and Training: Issues and Alternatives," Project Report. Washington, D.C.: U.S. Department of Education, National Center for Education Statistics, 1983a.

— "Post-Compulsory Education and Training: An Inventory of Programs and Sources of Support," in H. Levin and H.G. Schütze, (eds) Financing Recurrent Education, op. cit (Wagner 1983 b).

— "Research and Policy Issues in Financial Aid for the Independent and Adult Student," unpublished manuscript. Albany, NY: State University of New York at Albany, 1983c.

— "An (Almost) Sure Bet: The Payoff to a College Degree," unpublished manuscript. Albany, NY: State University of New York at Albany, 1984.

Wagner, Alan P. and Nancy Carlson. *Defining Independence Financial Aid for Self-Supporting Students*. Washington, D.C.: The College Board, 1983.

Windham, Douglas M. "On Theory and Policy in Financing Lifelong Learning," *School Review* 86 (May 1978): 535-43.

— "The Benefits and Financing of American Higher Education: Theory, Research, and Policy," *IFG Project Report* No. 80-A19. Stanford: Institute for Research on Educational Finance and Governance, November 1980.

Zemsky, R., ed. *Trainings Benchmarks A Statistical Sketch of Employer-Provided Training and Education 1963—1981*. Philadelphia, The University of Pennsylvania, 1983.

Adults in higher education: The situation in Canada

by
Pierre Paquet

TABLE OF CONTENTS

	Page
Chapter I. "Adult Students" in First Degree Programs	125
A Background: The Higher Education System	125
1. Institutions and Enrolments	128
a) The University: A Definition of Terms	128
b) Higher Education Institutions	128
Number of Institutions	128
Size of Institutions	129
Language of Instruction	129
Principal Characteristics of the Canadian University System	132
c) University Enrolments	133
An Overview	133
Distribution of Enrolment by Age	133
Distribution of Enrolment by Sex	136
Distribution by Souid origin	136
Distribution of Enrolment by Type of Attendance	137
2. Admission	138
3. First Degree Programs	140
4. Organization of Studies	140
5. Financing of Higher Education Institutions	141
a) Expenditures	141
b) Revenues	142
c) University Grant Calculation Formulae	142
6. Financing Tuition and Living Accommodation Costs	144
a) Loans and Bursaries	144
b) Interest Rates	145
c) Interest Relief Plans	145
d) Tax Exemptions	145
e) Exemptions From Payment of Student Fees	145
B. Characteristics of "Adult Students" in First Degree Programs	146
1. Adult Participation in the Education System	146
2. "Adult Students" in Universities	146
a) by Age	146
b) by Sex	148
c) by Field of Study	149
3. Other Variables Related to Type of Attendance	149
a) Social Origin	149
b) Paid Employment	149
c) Other Variables	152

C. Policies and Practices of Higher Education Institutions
  Concerning Adult Students   152
   1. Admission Requirements   152
   2. Evaluation Options   153
   3. Attendance Options   154
      a) Athabasca University (Alberta)   154
      b) Télé-université (Québec)   155
      c) Open Learning Institute (British Columbia)   155
   4. Availability of Information Concerning
      First Degree Programs   155
   5. Counselling and Guidance Services in
      First Degree Programs   156
   6. Placement Services in First Degree Programs   156
D. Financial Provisions: Modes of Financing for Mature Students   157
   1. Loans and Bursaries   157
   2. Scholarships   161
   3. The Canada Manpower Training Program   161
   4. Paid Employment   162
   5. Tax Exemptions Ajpplicable to Students   162
   6. Payment of Tuition Fees by Employer   162
   7. Tax Exemptions Applicable to Enterprises   163
   8. Educational Leave   163
E. Attitudes Concerning Adult Participation in First Degree Programs 164
   1. Institutions   164
   2. Employers   164
   3. Government   165

Chapter II. Adults in Continuing Education Activities Provided
            by Universities and Higher Education Insitutions   166
A. Background: Academic and Non-Academic Institutions That Provide
  Continuing Education   166
   1. Institutions and Enrolments   166
      a) Institutions   166
      b) Enrolments   168
   2. Programs of Study   170
      a) In Universities   170
      b) In Industry   170
      c) In Labour Organizations   171
   3. Organization   172
      a) In Universities   172
      b) In Industry   172
      c) In Labour Organizations   173

		Page
4. Financing Programs		173
a) In Universities		173
b) In Industry		174
c) In Labour Organizations		174
5. Financing Tuition and Living Accommodation Costs		175
B. Characteristics of Students in Continuing Education Activities		175
1. Participation in Continuing Education by Age		175
2. Participation in Continuing Education by Sex		175
3. Participation in Continuing Education by Educational Attainment		175
4. Participation in Continuing Education by Income		176
5. Participation in Continuing Education by Occupation		176
Conclusion		176
Bibliography		178

Chapter I
"Adult students" in first degree programs

A. BACKGROUND: THE HIGHER EDUCATION SYSTEM

"In 1976, the External Examiners appointed by the Organization for Economic Co-operation and Development expressed the following view on education policy and the Canadian constitution:
"Officially, there is no Federal presence in the area of educational policy, and the Federal Government behaves (at least in public) as if there were none ... In reality, though, the educational policies of the Federal government, and the financial concomitants of that policy, cannot be overlooked. A considerable Federal presence in educational policy is indeed tolerated by the Provinces and arouses no hostility, as long as nobody calls it educational policy, and as long as there are no overt strings attached to money coming from Ottawa.
"This 'Do-One-Thing-As-If-It-Were-Something-Else' attitude does not please all Canadians, some of whom describe it as 'intolerable' and 'almost schizophrenic'. But to some extent, behaviour that strikes outsiders as elaborate make-believe may, in fact, be a necessary price, willingly paid, to hold together a political confederation of disparate Provinces — and therefore understandable and even functional." (CAAE-ICEA, 1982:23)

This opinion of the OECD external examiners underlines one of the principal features of the context in which this report has been produced. Canada is a confederation of ten provinces. Each province, under the Constitution, is responsible within its own territory for the development of its education system from junior kindergarten to university. That is why, as an observer noted in a study of the Canadian university system:

One cannot expect the provincial governments to offer a spontaneous welcome to new federal initiatives in postsecondary education. All the provinces are leery of federal intrusions into areas which they consider to be exclusively within their own

125

jurisdiction, and education occupies a virtually unique place as the subject of provincial jealousy." (Leslie, 1980:402)

And yet, the federal government plays a substantial role in the field of education, in particular through funding:

"By 1981, federal educational expenditure had reached a level of $5.7 billion, of which more than $5 billion went toward the education of persons beyond the compulsory scchool leaving age in each of the Canadian jurisdictions.
"Among the federal interventions in education, three are key to the present state of adult education:
- post-secondary transfers to the provinces
- student loans
- occupational training." (CAAE-ICEA, 1982:23)

Another important dimension of the Canadian mosaic is the privileged position held by the two founding nations, one of French, and one of English origin. Over time, they have built this country which both claims and wishes to be bilingual. English and French are Canada's two official languages. 80 % francophones. Out of a total of 24.3 million inhabitants (according to the 1981 census), a little over 60 % have English as their mother tongue and 25 % have French as their mother tongue. In view of this, it is understandable that linguistic and cultural issues occupy an important place in Canadian political life.

Because of such constitutional and cultural circumstances, everything that affects education touches a sensitive nerve, even when it is labelled training in an attempt to establish distinctions whose validity we do not propose to question.

Canadians have learned to live with this reality (which has often had its capricious and, at times, thorny side) by trying to make the best of it. The report released in March, 1984 by the National Advisory Panel on Skill Development Leave (*Learning for Life*) shows that, in many cases, this approach has a positive and dynamic effect. At the federal l level, the Secretary of State is responsible for matters concerning education and, hence, for relations with the provinces in this area. On the other hand, the ten provinces have established the Council of Ministers of Education to facilitate cooperation among themselves, with the federal government, and with other organizations involved in education. (cf. Diagram 1 for the of governance of higher education in Canada).

This brief description of the Canadian socio-political and cultural context helps us to understand the following statement taken from the *Directory of Canadian Universities*, published by the Association of Universities and Colleges of Canada:

"There is a limit to the extent to which one can generalize about the Canadian universities on a country-wide basis. Each provincial system has its particular characteristics and its unique institutions." (AUCC, 1982:32)

Diagram 1: Framework of Higher Education

Jurisdiction	Government Departments	Other Government Agencies	University Collectivity
Federal	Secretary of State MOSST Department of Finance	NSERC SSHRC MRC NRC Stats Can	Association Universities & Colleges of Canada
National	Council of Ministers of Education, Canada		
NEWFOUNDLAND	Department of Education		
PRINCE EDWARD ISLAND	Department of Education	Maritime Provinces Higher Education Commission	Association of Atlantic Universities
NOVA SCOTIA	Department of Education / Council of Maritime Premiers		
NEW BRUNSWICK	Premier's Office		
QUÉBEC	Ministère de l'Enseignement Supérieur, de la Science et de la Technologie[2]	Conseil des universités	CREPUQ[1]
ONTARIO	Ministry of Colleges and Universities	Ontario Council on University Affairs	Council of Ontario Universities
MANITOBA	Department of Education	Manitoba Universities Grants Commission	
SASKATCHEWAN	Department of Advanced Education and Manpower		Council of Western Canadian University Presidents
ALBERTA	Department of Advanced Education		
BRITISH COLUMBIA	Ministry of Universities, Sciences & Communications	Universities Council of British Columbia	

[1] Conference of Rectors and Principals of Quebec Universities
[2] The name of the Ministry changed as corrected, as of 1985.

Source: AUCC, Ottawa. Compendium of University Statistics. Ottawa, 1983, P.1.

1. Institutions and Enrolments

a) The University: A Definition of Terms

"In Canada, a post-secondary educational institution having the power to grant degrees, is usually called a university. However, several of these institutions are called colleges, a few are known as institutes and one is a school.

"A university or college may be associated with another university, often called a 'parent' university, as a federated, affiliated or constituent institution. A federated institution is responsible for its own administration and has the power to grant degrees. While in federation, it holds some or all of its degree-conferring power in abeyance. An affiliated institution, usually a college, is responsible for its own administration, but does not have the power to grant degrees. In both cases, the parent university supervises instruction in the programs covered by the federation or affiliation agreement, and grants degrees to the students who successfully complete those programs. A constituent university or college is an integral part of the parent university with respect to both administrative and academic matters.

"A college may be a university-level institution with or without the power to grant degrees. In some cases, a college is a subdivision of a university: a teaching unit or a residence, or a combination of the two. And the term college is now commonly used for an institution which offers post-secondary courses for transfer to university, or courses which are occupationally oriented, or both, e.g. a community college." (AUCC, 1982:i)

Four provinces, namely, Ouébec, British Columbia, Alberta, and Saskatchewan, have institutions within their community college sector offering courses for transfer to university (i.e., university-level courses) (1). These courses correspond to the first year and sometimes to the first two years of a first degree program.

The data presented in this report deal only with university-level institutions as such, and do not take community colleges into account.

b) Higher Education Institutions

The Association of Universities and Colleges of Canada (2) publishes a directory (AUCC, 1982) which is a mine of information on the university system in Canada. In another of its publications (AUCC, 1983:1), the AUCC provides a diagram (reproduced on the following page) which gives an overview of the organization of the university system in Canada.

Number of Institutions

With one exception (3), all universities have been established by provincial legislatures:

"Universities are incorporated by provincial legislation, and with their own charters (properly called acts of incorporation), their own governing boards, the right to decide what shall be taught, who shall teach, who may be admitted to study and who may be granted degrees. In addition, they may decide how to spend their income. (CMEC, 1981:37)

128

Table 1 demonstrates that the number of university-level institutions varies from one province to another. Two provinces (Newfoundland and Prince Edward Island) have only one university each. On the other hand, about a third of Canadian universities are located in Ontario, which also has one third (35 %) of Canada's population according to the 1981 census. Québec, with 26 % of Canada's population, accounts for 10 % of all university-level institutions. The Atlantic provinces (Newfoundland, Prince Edward Island, Nova Scotia, and New Brunswick), with less than 10 % of Canada's population, account for one quarter of all universities.

Table 1 also draws attention to one of the characteristics of the university system in Canada: a large proportion of the institutions grant advanced degrees. Only five of the 66 universities are limited to granting first degrees.

Size of Institutions
The universities are of varying size and complexity. Some of them have more than 20,000 full-time students grouped within a dozen colleges, faculties or schools (two of the 68 universities), whereas others admit less than, 1,000 full-time students (22 of the 66 universities). See Table 2.

A report of the Council of Ministers of Education on post-secondary education divided universities into three categories, as follows:

> "(a) large universities in metropolitan centres, offering av wide range of opportunities for professional training and for graduate studies and research, (b) smaller universities in smaller centres, offering a more restricted range of studies, (c) even smaller institutions, often in rural settings, offering undergraduate programs only." (CMEC, 1981:14)

There facts indicate the diversity of situations in the different provinces. The author of an exhaustive study of the Canadian university system, views this as:

> "reflecting differences between then in culture, in population size and distribution, and in the financial resources of provincial governments. . . . The diversity one observes is a legacy of past decisions and also to some extent, expresses preferences which may hold long into the future." (Leslie, 1980:73)

Language of Instruction
Another variable which enables us to differentiate between the universities is the bilingual nature of Canada. As we have already mentioned, French is the mother tongue for 25.7 % of the Canadian population. University programs in all of the disciplines offered are available in English in each of the ten provinces. As for university programs offered in French outside of Ouébec, a report of the Council of Ministers of Education has expressed the following view of the matter:

> "While it is true that a general university course in arts and a degree course in education can be followed in French, or largely in French, in six of the other nine provinces, other professional training programs in French are available only in two of them (New Brunswick and Ontario). Non-degree programs in French are even fewer. To compensate, in part, for the relatively few educational institutions outside

Ouébec which use French as the medium of instruction, the federal government provides bursaries which assist French-speaking students to travel to institutions in which they can study in that language." (CMEC, 1981:7)

Table 1
UNIVERSITY-LEVEL INSTITUTIONS BY TYPE: CANADA AND PROVINCES, 1983–1984

	Universities with		Universities and Other Degree-Granting Institutions				Total
	Undergraduate programs only	Undergraduate and master's programs	Undergraduate, master's and doc-toral programs	Colleges of Theology	Liberal Arts Colleges	Other	
Newfoundland	—	—	1	—	—	—	1
Prince Edward Island	—	1	—	—	—	—	1
Nova Scotia	1	4	1	1	1	2	10
New Brunswick	1	2	1	—	—	—	4
Québec	—	1	6	—	—	—	7
Ontario	—	6	10	4	—	1	21
Manitoba	1	1	1	4	—	—	7
Saskat chewan	—	—	2	2	—	—	4
Alberta	2	—	2	1	—	—	5
British Columbia	—	—	3	2	1	—	6
Canada	5	15	27	14	2	3	66

Source: Statistics Canada, Ottawa. *Education in Canada: 1983–84.* Ottawa, July 1985, Table 14, pp. 74–75. (Catalogue 81–229 Annual).

Table 2
UNIVERSITY-LEVEL INSTITUTIONS BY SIZE OF FULL-TIME ENROLMENT: CANADA AND PROVINCES, 1983–1984

	Size of Universities and Other Degree-Granting Institutions										
	99—	100—299	300—499	500—999	1,000—2,999	3,000—4,999	5,000—9,999	10,000—19,999	20,000—29,999	30,000 and up	Total
Newfoundland	—	—	—	—	—	—	1	—	—	—	1
Prince Edward Island	—	—	—	—	1	—	—	—	—	—	1
Nova Scotia	1	1	2	1	1	3	1	—	—	—	10
New Brunswick	—	—	—	—	2	1	1	—	—	—	4
Québec	—	—	—	1	—	—	1	4	1	—	7
Ontario	—	3	1	1	1	4	3	6	1	1	21
Manitoba	1	3	—	—	2	—	—	1	—	—	7
Saskatchewan	—	1	1	—	—	—	1	1	—	—	4
Alberta	2	—	—	—	1	—	—	1	1	—	5
British Columbia	1	1	—	1	—	—	2	—	1	—	6
Canada	5	9	4	4	8	8	10	13	4	1	66

Source: Statistics Canada, Ottawa. *Education in Canada: 1983–84.* Ottawa, July 1985, Table 15, pp. 78–79 (Catalogue 81–229 Annual).

Principal Characteristics of the Canadian University System

Despite the diversity of our university system, one can try to identify the principal characteristics that distinguish it from systems in other countries. A set of features which, taken individually, are not distinctive, can be used to identify the "unique" character of Canadian universities.

An overview of this kind is to be found in Leslie's study referred to above. A summary of his description is given below:

> "Canadian educational authorities — in government and out of it — have been declared advocates of equal standards of achievment. They have shrunk from any suggestion that public policy ought to establish a hierarchy of institutions in terms of quality, and to accord favoured treatment to the front runners.

> ". . . relatively few universities have restricted themselves to undergraduate teaching, or are so restricted by charter or founding legislation. . . . Doctoral work was conducted on thirty university campuses — rather more than half the total, representing more than 85 per cent of the aggregate number of full-time university-level students.

> ". . . A third feature of Canadian higher education is the combination of teaching and research functions in the university. This works well, and it appears to improve the quality of both. It is also in keeping with the Anglo-American tradition, though it contrasts with practice in some continental European countries, notably France.

> ". . . A final observation about the structure of Canadian higher education is that there is no longer any differentiation of universities by source of funds. Formerly, churchsupported or other private institutions, with the exception of some theological colleges or universities, have acquired quasi-public status. Traditions of private benefaction have never developed in Canada to the same extent as they have in the United States; indeed, now that the state has assumed so many responsibilities in education, health care, and social services, private support is considerably weaker than previously it was. It is now probably impossible for any Canadian universities to free themselves from financial dependency on the public purse, if indeed this ever was an option. Thus, the wealthy private university, which is so important a feature of higher education in the United States, does not exist in Canada. The private-public distinction does not apply." (Leslie, 1980:61—64)

Another feature which characterizes the Canadian university system as a whole (without necessarily distinguishing it from university systems in other countries) is related to the stated objective of facilitating access of the entire population to higher education. A report prepared by the Council of Ministers of Education for the OECD observed:

> "Governments and institutions alike are intent on providing equality of opportunity for post-secondary education in spite of disadvantages which may be related to (1) location, (2) sex, (3) ethnicity, (4) physical condition, (5) social status, and (6) financial resources. To be more direct, though perhaps to oversimplify, these disadvantages being non-white, being handicapped, having parents with little schooling, and being poor." (CMEC, 1981:15)

Over the past two decades, considerable efforts and resources have been deployed to increase equality of opportunity for post-secondary education, notably through decentralizing educational activities and expanding the range of methods used to transmit knowledge. Some provinces:

">. . . have provided most of their regions with universities. Some aid is available to meet the additional costs incurred by students at institutions beyond commuting range.
">. . . In more provinces, distance learning facilities have been established to serve people living in thinly populated areas." (CMEC, 1981:5–6)

c. University Enrolments

An Overview

The Directory of Universities published by the AUCC describes the general situation as follows:

"Of the students who complete secondary school in Canada, about 50 per cent continue in some form of full-time postsecondary education, roughly half of these, i.e., 25 per cent of high school graduates, entering university. Women slightly outnumber men in faculties of arts and science and predominate in such professional faculties as education, household science, nursing, rehabilitation medicine, secretarial science and social work. But men are more numerous in faculties of architecture, commerce, dentistry, engineering, forestry, medicine, and theology, and in graduate studies. Of students who qualify for a first degree, about one in five goes on for an advanced degree." (AUCC, 1982:iii)

What are the numbers that correspond to the ratios presented by the AUCC? The latest "final" statistics available are for the 1983–84 academic year. During this period, 729,231 people were enrolled in universities in Canada (642,163 at the undergraduate level and 87,068 at the graduate level). Table 3 illustrates the breakdown of these figures by province (4).

This table demonstrates the fact that 68 % of the students are concentrated in the two central provinces (Ontario and Ouébec). The four Atlantic provinces (Newfoundland, Prince Edward Island, Nova Scotia and New Brunswick) account for 9 %, and the western provinces for 23 %.

Distribution of Enrolment by Age

The age classification of students enrolled in universities at the undergraduate level, in 1983–84, indicates the important position held by "adult students". More than a third of the students are 25 or older and, in this category, four out of five students are between 25 and 39 years of age. Table 4 illustrates the distribution of students by age group in each of the provinces.

Table 4 highlights the particular situation in Ouébec, where 51.5 % of students enrolled in universities are 25 or older. On the other hand, only one quarter of the students attending university in Nova Scotia could be classified as "adult students".

Table 3

UNIVERSITY ENROLMENT BY LEVEL: CANADA AND PROVINCES, 1983–1984

	Undergraduate		Graduate		Total	
	Number	*Per Cent*	*Number*	*Per Cent*	*Number*	*Per Cent*
Newfoundland	11,140	1.7	1,027	1.2	12,167	1.7
Prince Edward Island	2,385	0.4	—	—	2,385	0.3
Nova Scotia	26,548	4.1	2,938	3.4	29,486	4.0
New Brunswick	17,775	2.8	1,144	1.3	18,919	2.6
Québec	183,128	28.5	29,508	33.9	212,636	29.2
Ontario	248,244	38.7	32,718	37.6	280,962	38.5
Manitoba	31,175	4.9	4,076	4.7	32,251	4.8
Saskatchewan	26,266	4.1	1,711	2.0	27,977	3.8
Alberta	49,498	7.7	6,730	7.7	56,228	7.7
British Columbia	44,004	7.2	7,216	8.3	53,220	7.3
Canada	642,163	100.0	87,068	100.0	729,231	100.0

Source: Statistics Canada, Ottawa. *Advance Statistics of Education.* Ottawa, September 1985, Table 8–9, pp. 25–26 (Catalogue 81–220 Annual).

Table 4
UNDERGRADUATE UNIVERSITY ENROLMENT BY AGE: CANADA AND PROVINCES, 1983–1984

	Less than 20 years	20–24 years	25–29 years	30–39 years	40 years and over	25 years and over	TOTAL NUMBER
				Number			
Newfoundland	3,508	4,192	1,174	1,693	573	3,440	11,140
Prince Edward I.	807	888	217	268	200	685	2,380
Nova Scotia	7,598	12,001	2,661	2,415	1,308	6,384	25,983
New Brunswick	5,574	7,238	1,808	1,979	998	4,785	17,597
Québec	11,384	76,917	33,268	39,509	21,061	93,838	182,139
Ontario	39,046	127,891	29,876	32,303	18,505	80,684	247,621
Manitoba	8,073	13,616	3,829	3,493	1,817	9,139	30,828
Saskatchewan	6,447	10,844	3,711	3,603	1,510	8,824	26,115
Alberta	10,875	21,072	7,868	6,947	2,706	17,521	49,468
British Columbia	9,585	20,577	6,643	5,591	2,542	14,776	44,938
Canada	102,897	295,236	91,055	97,801	51,220	240,076	638,209
				Percentage			
Newfoundland	31.5	37.6	10.5	15.2	5.1	30.9	100.0
Prince Edward I.	33.9	37.5	9.1	11.3	8.4	28.8	100.0
Nova Scotia	29.2	46.2	10.2	9.3	5.0	24.6	100.0
New Brunswick	31.7	41.1	10.3	11.2	5.7	27.2	100.0
Québec	6.3	42.2	18.3	21.7	11.6	51.5	100.0
Ontario	15.8	51.6	12.1	13.0	7.5	32.6	100.0
Manitoba	26.2	44.2	12.4	11.3	5.9	29.6	100.0
Saskatchewan	24.7	41.5	14.2	13.8	5.8	33.8	100.0
Alberta	22.0	42.6	15.9	14.0	5.5	35.4	100.0
British Columbia	21.3	45.8	14.8	12.4	5.7	32.9	100.0
Canada	16.1	46.3	14.3	15.3	8.0	37.6	100.0

Source: This table was prepared on the basis of information obtained from: Statistics Canada, Ottawa, *Universities: Enrolment and Degrees*. Ottawa, September 1985, Table 15, pp. 36–37 (Catalogue 81–204 Annual).

In the under-20 student category, equally significant differences can be found between the provinces. The two central provinces (Ontario and Ouébec) account for a lesser proportion of students under 20 years of age in comparison with the other provinces. Conversely, the proportion of students under the age of 20 in Newfoundland and in Prince Edward Island is almost twice the national average. These somewhat astonishing results show to what extent student age groups at the university level are affected by the particular organization of the post-secondary education system in each of the provinces. In Ouébec and Ontario, students must complete 13 years of schooling before entering university, whereas, until very recently, students in Newfoundland entered university after 11 years of schooling (5).

Distribution of Enrolment by Sex

During the last 15 years, the proportion of women among university students increased remarkably, so that in 1983—84, there were slightly more women than men enrolled at the undergraduate level. As illustrated in Table 5, this situation holds true for each of the provinces. At this level, the disparity between the provinces is relatively slight.

Table 5
UNDERGRADUATE UNIVERSITY ENROLMENT BY SEX:
CANADA AND PROVINCES, 1983–1984

	Total Number	Men Per Cent	Women Per Cent
Newfoundland	11,140	45.3	54.7
Prince Edward Island	2,385	43.7	56.3
Nova Scotia	26,548	48.5	51.5
New Brunswick	17,775	48.5	51.5
Québec	183,128	47.0	53.0
Ontario	248,244	47.9	52.1
Manitoba	31,175	47.9	52.1
Saskatchewan	26,266	47.7	52.3
Alberta	49,498	48.0	52.0
British Columbia	44,004	48.8	51.2
Canada	642,163	47.7	53.2

Source: Statistics Canada, Ottawa, *Advance Statistics of Education.* Ottawa, September 1985, Table 8—9, pp. 25—26 (Catalogue 81—220 Annual).

Distribution of Enrolment by Social Origin

According to Paul Anisef who, over the last few years, has conducted a variety of research studies into the social origins of students, research in Canada has yet to attain the depth of James Coleman's work in the United States. Nevertheless, various studies have analysed access to higher education and the social origins of students attending post-secondary institutions in Ontario and Québec.

Also, as noted in the report of the Federal-Provincial Task Force on Student Assistance:

"While there are no consistent national readings on changes in the composition of the post-secondary education population with respect to the socio-economic background of the student's family, enough separate studies have been conducted to make it quite clear that lower socio-economic status groups have been and still are considerably underrepresented. . . . What evidence is available on changes over time is discouraging. For example, Max von Zur-Muehlen ("The Educational Background of Parents of Post-Secondary Students in Canada", March 1, 1978) compared data on parents' educational attainment (a reasonably good measure of socio-economic status" between 1968−69 and 1974−75. In this period, the author found that there had been a tendency to greater inequality of educational opportunity at the university level although, in absolute numbers, all social classes shared in the expansion of access to post-secondary education that took place during this period." (Federal-Provincial Task Force on Student Assistance, 1981:97)

Considerable resources were allocated to education in the 1970s. Nevertheless, Paul Anisef's review of studies on social class and access to education in Ontario led him to conclude:

". . . there is little evidence . . . that educational expansion has succeeded in reducing existing social class differentials . . . Peter M. Leslie, in a recent policy study for the Association of Universities and Colleges of Canada . . . admits that the present fiscal-crisis mentality of government can bring 'hardship to academically talented young people whose life chances depend on their having access to university education of the highest quality'." (Anisef, 1983:39)

At this same conference, which was organized by the Council of Ministers of Education in 1982, one of the panelists stated that the action taken by governments to overcome obstacles related to social origin was "rather ineffectual":

"The action undertaken so far has assisted in the advancement of all social classes without reducing the inequalities between classes . . . The educational level of all Canadians has risen by a notch, but the gaps due to 'social status' and 'financial resources' have not been closed." (Bertrand, 1983:60)

As was pointed out in the Faure Report (UNESCO-OISE, 1973:72): "Equal access is different from equal opportunity. Equal access cannot respond to social inequality, while equal opportunity can only be understood as the 'opportunity to succeed', and such chances are, in fact, very unequal".

Distribution of Enrolment by Type of Attendance
Part-time studies have developed steadily over the past 20 years. In 1964, part-time enrolment at universities represented 26 % of the student population. During the last two decades, the relative importance of part-time students has greatly increased. According to the most recent data available, part-time students in Canada now represent 38 % of the total enrolment in university degree programs.

Table 6 illustrates the distribution of full-time and part-time students in each of the provinces for 1983−84.

This table highlights the rather significant differences between the provinces. In Québec, part-time students outnumber full-time students, but this is the only case where "tomorrow's majority" is a reality today (6). In two provinces (Nova Scotia and New Brunswick), part-time students still account for no more than about one-quarter of the total student population.

2. Admission

In most provinces, students enter university after completing 12 years of study (i.e., at the end of the secondary level). In Ontario and Québec, however, the completion of 13 years of schooling is required before admission to university. In Québec, this involves completing two years of a general course of study at the college level after the final secondary school year (i.e., grade 11). In Ontario, as a general rule, students who are preparing to enter university must have completed grade 13.

The *Directory of Canadian Universities* (AUCC) describes the general university entrance requirements af follows:

> "There is no Canada-wide entrance test or examination for admission to university; each university sets its own admission standards. The normal requirement for admission to a first-degree program in arts and science is a certificate of completion of secondary school for the province in which the university is located. In general, students applying for admission to the first year of a university program from outside the province in which the university is located would be considered eligible if they satisfy entrance requirements for admission to first year programs at universities in their home province, and can provide standards equivalent to those required of students eligible for admission and applying from within the province. Considerations include length of secondary program, academic standing, and evidence of a course of studies appropriate to the anticipated concentration at the university as set out in its calender.
>
> "In most cases, the universities require standing higher than the minimum necessary to qualify for the secondary school certificate (an average of 60 per cent, for example, rather than simply a pass of 50 per cent in each subject), and a pattern of subjects appropriate to the university program the student intends to follow.
>
> "Some professional degree programs may also be entered directly from secondary school. Examples are agriculture, engineering and pharmacy. Others require the applicant to have completed some or all of a first-degree program in arts or science. The minimum requirement for entry to dentistry, medicine or law, for example, may be two or more years of arts or science. In practice, however, a full degree is almost a necessity because competition for entry is keen. Still other professional faculties, e.g. library science, require a bachelor's degree in arts or science for entry." (AUCC, 1982:iv)

Moreover, in disciplines where demand exceeds available places (i.e., medicine, dentistry, veterinary medicine, business administration, accounting, computer science) the universities impose quotas on admissions, and tests are administered to facilitate the selection of candidates. In short, the universities have adopted a mixed system in which some disciplines are under a quota system, while others are unrestricted.

Table 6
UNIVERSITY ENROLMENT BY LEVEL AND REGISTRATION STATUS: CANADA AND PROVINCES, 1983–1984

	Undergraduate		Graduate		Total	
	Full-time	Part-time	Full-time	Part-time	Full-time	Part-time
	Number					
Newfoundland	7,409	3,731	618	409	8,027	4,140
Prince Edward Island	1,676	709	–	–	1,676	709
Nova Scotia	20,649	5,899	1,809	1,129	22,458	7,028
New Brunswick	13,460	4,315	695	449	14,155	4,764
Québec	87,552	95,576	16,300	13,208	103,852	108,784
Ontario	162,366	85,878	20,753	11,965	183,119	97,843
Manitoba	18,242	12,933	2,413	1,663	20,655	14,596
Saskatchewan	18,098	8,168	1,034	677	19,132	8,845
Alberta	35,670	13,828	4,540	2,190	40,210	16,018
British Columbia	32,227	13,777	5,020	2,196	37,247	15,973
Canada	397,349	244,814	53,182	33,886	450,531	278,700
	Per Cent					
Newfoundland	66.5	33.5	60.2	39.8	66.0	34.0
Prince Edward Island	70.3	29.7	–	–	70.3	29.7
Nova Scotia	77.8	22.2	61.1	38.4	76.2	23.8
New Brunswick	75.7	23.4	60.8	39.2	74.8	25.2
Québec	47.8	52.2	55.2	44.8	48.8	51.2
Ontario	65.4	34.6	63.4	36.6	65.2	34.8
Manitoba	58.5	41.5	59.2	40.8	58.6	41.4
Saskatchewan	68.9	31.1	60.4	39.6	68.4	31.6
Alberta	72.1	27.9	67.5	32.5	71.5	28.5
British Columbia	70.1	29.9	69.6	30.4	70.0	30.0
Canada	61.9	38.1	61.1	38.9	61.8	38.2

Source: Statistics Canada, Ottawa, *Advance Statistics of Education*. Ottawa September 1985, Table 8, pp. 25–26 (Catalogue 81–220 Annual).

All universities admit foreign students, but here too:

> "Some universities impose quotas on the number of foreign students who may be admitted to certain faculties, especially those offering professional degree programs." (AUCC, 1982:v)

3. *First Degree Programs* (7)

Undergraduate, graduate. Undergraduate programs of study include those leading to a bachelor's or first professional degree, as well as to diplomas and certificates below degree level. Graduate, sometimes called postgraduate, programs lead to advanced degrees, diplomas and certificates for which a first degree is a prerequisite. Students in undergraduate programs are called undergraduates; those in graduate programs, graduate students.

Program, course, subject. A program of study, e.g., one leading to a bachelor's degree in arts, is a patterned combination and sequence of courses in a variety of subjects. . . . A general program of studies leading to a bachelor's degree in arts or science requires a minimum of three years from secondary school graduation, an honours program usually four. Programs leading to a first professional degree vary in length and take, depending on the discipline and university, from three to five years either from secondary school graduation or after two or three years of general academic study . . . The honours program . . . requires higher standing for admission and for the maintenance of honour status.

The normal course load of a full-time undergraduate in arts and science is five subjects studied concurrently, each involving a minimum of three hours of class time a week. Two hours of lectures and one of tutorial is a common pattern in non-science subjects. To these is likely to be added a three-hour laboratory class each week in each science subject and the equivalent in oral-language subjects, accounting and others in which experiment, problem-solving or practice are required. Students in professional schools are scheduled for as many as 30 hours of instruction a week. In all cases, it is customary to compress these hours into five days a week, Monday to Friday.

First-degree programs in the liberal arts — humanities, social sciences, life sciences, and physical sciences — are provided by all but a few specialized institutions. In addition, most universities have programs in which students may prepare for entry to the professions — the traditional ones, law, medicine and theology, and a host of others of more recent origin. Some of the larger universities provide almost the full range of professional studies, but specialization in a smaller number is more often the rule. Opportunities for general, and sometimes professional, continuing education are provided by almost all universities.

4. *Organization of Studies*

One of the most common ways of increasing accessibility to postsecondary education is through part-time studies. In 1983–84, 38 % of the students enrolled in universities were using this method to reconcile the demands of school and work. Part-time studies are accessible to "adults" because courses are offered outside of normal working hours (in the late afternoon, in the evening, or on weekends).

The introduction of other combinations, which have rather been aimed at full-time students, has further increased the array of course organization methods.

Some 20 universities:

> "... organize studies in some faculties on what is called the cooperative plan, alternating full-time study on campus during one term with full-time employment providing supervised work experience (and pay) during the next ...
> "Cooperative work/study schemes, which operate on a year-round basis, were first offered in engineering, but are now available in other disciplines. Other year-round programs are provided mainly by faculties of arts and science." (AUCC, 1982:iv)

Whereas, under normal circumstances, the university year consists of two four-month terms (September to December and January to April), some universities:

> "... provide for year-round operation with three terms or semesters, the third running from May to August ... Where there is a three-term or trimester calendar, students may enrol for any one, two or three terms in a 12-month period: the trimester system allows the students to graduate in less than the usual number of years. Its flexibility also permits students to catch up if they have fallen out of step with the normal rate of progress." (AUCC, 1982:iii-iv)

This method of decreasing the time period required to obtain a degree could motivate some people to return to school, since the total duration of courses would be somewhat reduced by such a formula.

To facilitate access for people who cannot take part in educational activities on a university campus for such reasons as lack of time, too great a distance from educational institutions or insufficient funds, the so-called "traditional" universities have introduced various new approaches. These include:

- Off-campus activities that are organized on a regular basis or as a response to specific needs.
- Permanent centres in remote regions offering learning activities on a regular basis.
- In at least one case, the university is made up of a network of permanent regional centres offering a wide range of programs.
- Correspondence courses (8).

In addition, "non-traditional" institutions mandated to provide or facilitate learning at a distance have been established in various Provinces. Such institutions have been founded, in particular in British Columbia (Knowledge Network, Open Learning Institute), in Alberta (Athabasca University, ACCESS), in Ontario (TV Ontario), and in Québec (Télé-université, Radio Québec).

5. Financing of Higher Education Institutions

a) Expenditures

As illustrated in Table 7a total 1985−86 expenditures by Canadian universities will amount to a little more than $6.5 billion ($6,521,000,000). This amounts to 19.6 % of total expenditures for the educational system at all levels in Canada. Table 7b indicates the allocation of operating expenditures, by function and type, in Canadian universities in 1983−84. This second chart shows that approximately three-quarters of the operating expenditures in universities are

141

allocated to salaries and benefits for various categories of employees.

b)   Revenues

"Under the Post-Secondary Education Financing Program, the Secretary of State makes unconditional payments to provincial and territorial governments in support of postsecondary education. This program is one of three established programs included under Part VI of the Federal-Provincial Fiscal Arrangements and Established Programs Financing Act, 1977, as amended in 1982. The other two programs relate to medicare and hospital insurance." (Secretary of State, 1983b:14)

In official statistics, the amounts corresponding to tax transfer points are attributed to the provinces. For the 1983—84 fiscal year, the credits allocated to provinces under the Post-Secondary Education Financing Program (college and university levels) totalled $3.97 billion ($1.95 billion in direct cash transfers and $2.02 billion in tax point transfers). (Statistics Canada, 1985c:3—4)

The source of funds allocated to universities in 1985—86, as illustrated in Table 7a, shows the considerable portion of university revenues that comes from government sources (92 %), and in particular from the provincial governments (66 %). Over the years, the involvment of governments, especially provincial governments, has taken on a major dimension.

Table 7a
SOURCES OF FUNDS AND EXPENDITURES FOR EDUCATION, CANADA, 1985–86

Sources of funds	Sum in Million $	%
Provincial and Territorial Governments	22.090	66.2
Municipal Governments	5.522	16.6
Federal Government	2.991	9.0
Non-Government (Private) Sources	2.733	8.2
Total	33.336	100

Expenditures	Sum in Million $	%
Elementary and Secondary Schools	21.927	65.8
University	6.521	19.5
Community College	2.560	7.6
Vocational Training	2.328	7.0
Total	33.336	100

Source: Statistics Canada, Ottawa, *Statistics of Education.* Ottawa, September 1985, Chart 6, p. 17 (Catalogue 81—220 Annual).

". . . Governments have a great deal of potential power over the universities. The fact that they use that potential sparingly may be attributed to the long tradition of university autonomy and the appreciation by governments of the effectiveness of free institutions. Nevertheless, as governments become aware of the need for rationalization of university program offerings, and the slowness with which the universities respond to that need, the political authorities feel obliged to exert their influence. This they do by controlling capital expenditures and the introduction of new programs. The next stage is to eliminate some present programs, but this is difficult and seldom achieved." (CMEC, 1981:37−38)

An analysis of "direct" funding sources shows that in 1983−84 governments provide approximately 80 % of university financing while student fees and other sources contribute about 10 % each. Student fees, which were formerly a major source of revenue, are now proportionately much less important. (Statistics Canada, 1985d:5)

Table 7b
PERCENTAGE DISTRIBUTION OF UNIVERSITY OPERATING EXPENDITURES, 1983–84

Total of expenditures		*$5.073,114,000*	
By Function			
Instruction	53.3 %	Physical Plant	10.7 %
Libraries	5.4	Student Services	2.4
Computing	2.8	Other	3.4
Administration	7.5	Sponsored Research	14.5
By Type			
Academic Ranks	33.7 %	Library Acquisitions	1.7 %
Other Salaries and Wages	28.1	Supplies and Expenses	8.5
Other Instruction and Resource	6.4	Furniture and Equipment	4.9
Fringe Benefits	7.8	Utilities and Taxes	3.5
		Miscellaneous	5.4

Source: Statistics Canada, Ottawa, *Education Statistics Bulletin*, 7 (3) August 1985, p. 8 (Catalogue 81−002).

c) University grant calculation formulae

Provincial governments are responsible for the allocation of grants to universities in their respective provinces. The following summarizes Leslie's description of the financing formulae:

"Existing funding practices in all provinces are a combination of three types of grants: discretionary grants, those determined by formula, and those allocated among universities according to historical ratios.

Discretionary grants are subsidies accorded to the university on the basis of the governments's judgment (or the judgment of a universities commission or other agent of the crown) as to what is necessary, or fair, or as generous as the condition of the public treasury will allow. Their magnitude is not determined by the application of proclaimed or acknowledged rules.

143

Formula financing is a way of determining the size of the provinces' operating subsidies, or some part of them, on the basis of an algebraic rule or formula. The formula may be used for two separate purposes: to determine how much the province will spend on the universities, and to determine in what proportions this sum, or a sum otherwise settled upon, will be distributed among them. At present, only Québec uses a formula which has any impact on government spending.

In the simpler formulae, such as those hitherto used in some Canadian provinces, *all* university costs are presumed to be proportional to those costs directly attribuable to instruction; thus, all that is needed to apply the formula is the total number of enrolment units for each institution. Each one's share of the available funds is the same as its share of the total number of enrolment units across the system." (Leslie, 1980:234—240)

6. *Financing Tuition and Living Accommodation Costs*

a) *Loans and Bursaries* (9)

"From the perspective of the post-secondary student, there are 12 quite different student assistance packages in Canada, one for each province and territory. In all provinces except Quebec, those packages include a mix of aid provided from the Federal government's Canada Student Loans Program (CSLP) and from provincial government loan, grant and/or bursary programs. Students cannot apply directly to the federal government for a CSLP loan; all programs are administered entirely by the provincial and territorial governments. Québec administers its own program which is similar to the other eleven.

The first step in seeking assistance under all 12 aid packages is for students to apply to a provincial or territorial government for aid and provide information about their financial resources and needs. The province or territory then determines the amount of aid for which the student is eligible, based on assessed financial need, and provides that aid whether as non-repayable grant or bursary (provided by provincial programs) or as an authorization for a guaranteed loan (either from the CSLP or a provincial loan program or both, or a mix of non-repayable and repayable aid). If the aid is in the form of an authorization for a guaranteed loan, the student then negotiates the loan at a bank or other commercial lending institution. The government responsible pays interest on the loan while the student is in school and for a short period thereafter, and guarantees repayment to the lending institution. There are a number of variations on this basic pattern. For example, in some provinces there are programs that forgive or remit part of the loan when a student graduates. British Columbia has a work-study element in its aid package.

While the 12 student aid packages are independently administered by the province or territory concerned, basic administratve criteria agreed to by the provinces and the federal government promote coordination. However, provinces may choose to use more stringent criteria in practice. A body known as the CSLP Plenary Group, composed of provincial, territorial, and federal officials, meets annually . . ."

Under the amendments introduced, in 1983, to the Canada Student Aid Act:

"Guaranteed loans for part-time students attending postsecondary courses are now available under a program funded by the Canadian government and administered by the provincial and territorial governments. The purpose of the plan is to make available guaranteed loans to needy part-time students to help cover the cost of tuition fees, books, learning materials, transportation, and related expenses." (Secretary of State, 1983a:20)

Provincial programs also provide limited bursaries to part-time students in four provinces (British Columbia, Alberta, Ontario and Québec).

The Canada Student Loans Program sets no age limit, neither for fulltime nor part-time students.

b)   Interest Rates

"During the period the student is in school, and for six months thereafter, the federal government pays interest on the student's CSLP loans. . . . There are two interest rates. One rate is payable by the federal government while the borrower is at school and for six months thereafter and a second rate is payable by the borrower after that period.

Three provinces, Alberta, Ontario and Québec, also provide loan assistance. Alberta determines maximum rates of interest using the same formula as that used by the federal government in the CSLP. Québec rates are similar except that they are averaged over three months and are changes quarterly rather than annually. The Ontario rates are based upon the prime lending rate of the bank advancing the loans rather than on a formula.

Experience with the formula approach has shown that the resulting rates have been, in general, well below commercial market rates and, hence, provide the student with a preferred rate." (Federal-Provincial Task Force on Student Assistance, 1981:111−112)

c)   Interest-Relief Plans

Also, as a result of amendments to the Student Aid Act:

"Starting on September 1, 1983, the Government of Canada will pay the interest on full- and part-time Canada Student Loans on behalf of debtors who are experiencing financial hardhip due to inability to find employment or to temporary disability." (Statistics Canada, 1983:11)

d)   Tax Exemptions (10)

"The tax system contributes significantly to resources from own employment and from parental contributions. The first $500 of scholarship and bursary income are exempt from tax (the federal value in terms of revenues not received was about $6 million in 1979). Students enrolled at designated educational institutions, mainly universities and colleges, full-time attendance. . . . Students may deduct their tuition fees for part-time courses or full-time enrolment at a college or university in computing their income for tax purposes."

e)   Exemptions from Payment of Student Fees

Some universities waive student fees in the case of senior citizens (i.e., persons over 60 or 65 years of age, according to the definition used by the university concerned).

145

B. CHARACTERISTICS OF "ADULT STUDENTS" IN FIRST DEGREE PROGRAMS

1. Adult Participation in the Education System

Using statistics from the last census, we can determine what percentage of adults 25 and over were full- or part-time students, at all levels, in Canada in 1981. In total, 11.7 % of the population (11) aged 15 years and older were full-time students, and 5.8 % (12) were part-time students.

The great majority (89.9 %) of full-time students consists of 15- to 24-year-olds; adults aged 25 years and older represent only one-tenth of the full-time student population. On the other hand, adults aged 25 years and older make up pracitically three-quarters of the total part-time student population. Part-time studies thus seem to be the main route by which adults reenter the educational system.

In Canada in 1981, the rate (13) of full-time school attendance at all levels among adults 25 years and older was 1.6 % (14). The rate of part-time attendance for the same category of student was 5.8 % (15). Practically speaking then, it can be said that four out of five adults (25 years and older) register in part-time studies when they return to school. This was the case at least, for the million adults who attended educational institutions, at all levels, in Canada in 1981.

2. "Adult Students" in Universities

How does the above-noted adult (25 years and over) participation in the educational system relate to the prevailing situation in the universities? In seeking to answer this question let ut note at the outset that statistics on "adult students" are not readily available. Furthermore, the majority of available statistics are based on type of attendance (full-time or part-time). To depict the situation in the universities, the latter criterion must be used. Our description will be based mainly on the type of attendance according to the age, sex, and field of study of those enrolled at the undergraduate level.

a) by Age

As we have seen, "adult students" now form a significant part of the university student population. People aged 25 and over account for 38 % of all students enrolled at the undergraduate level; part-time students also represent 38 % of university enrolment at the undergraduate level.

One might ask whether all "adult students" (25 and over) are enrolled part-time, or are rather divided between full-time and part-time studies. Table 8a shows that the actual situation in the universities reflects adult participation in the entire educational system, as illustrated by data collected for the 1981 census. In 1983−84, 14.3 % of the students enrolled full-time at the university level were 25 years or older, whereas 75.6 % of part-time students could be qualified as "adults" (according to the definition used in this report).

Table 8a
UNDERGRADUATE UNIVERSITY ENROLMENT BY REGISTRATION STATUS AND AGE: CANADA AND PROVINCES, 1983–1984

Full-Time

	Less than 20 years %	20–24 years %	25–29 years %	30–39 years %	40 years and over %	25 years and over %	Total Number
Newfoundland	44.8	44.5	6.7	3.2	0.9	10.7	7,409
Prince Edward Island	46.2	45.2	5.1	2.3	1.1	8.6	1,675
Nova Scotia	36.3	52.2	7.2	3.4	0.9	11.5	20,491
New Brunswick	40.7	48.5	7.2	2.9	0.8	10.9	13,426
Québec	12.5	68.5	12.6	5.3	1.0	18.9	87,140
Ontario	23.3	66.1	7.2	2.8	0.7	10.6	162,158
Manitoba	36.6	51.1	8.1	3.5	0.7	12.3	17,995
Saskatchewan	34.1	49.6	9.7	5.5	1.2	16.3	18,067
Alberta	28.6	51.5	12.4	6.0	1.5	19.9	35,652
British Columbia	28.2	53.5	11.5	5.6	1.2	18.3	31,408
Canada	24.7	61.1	9.3	4.0	0.9	14.3	395,421

Part-Time

	Less than 20 years %	20–24 years %	25–29 years %	30–39 years %	40 years and over %	25 years and over %	Total Number
Newfoundland	5.0	24.0	18.3	39.1	13.6	70.9	3,731
Prince Edward Island	4.7	18.6	18.6	32.5	25.7	76.7	705
Nova Scotia	2.9	23.9	21.5	31.3	20.4	73.2	5,492
New Brunswick	2.8	17.5	20.2	38.2	21.3	79.7	4,171
Québec	0.5	18.1	23.4	36.8	21.2	81.4	94,999
Ontario	1.5	24.3	21.3	32.6	20.3	74.2	85,463
Manitoba	11.5	34.5	18.5	22.3	13.2	54.0	12,833
Saskatchewan	3.6	23.4	24.3	32.5	16.1	73.0	8,048
Alberta	4.8	19.6	25.1	34.7	15.8	75.6	13,816
British Columbia	5.3	27.9	22.3	28.4	16.1	66.8	13,530
Canada	2.2	22.2	22.3	33.7	19.6	75.6	242,788

Source: This table was prepared on the basis of information obtained from: Statistics Canada, Ottawa, *Universities: Enrolment and Degrees.* Ottawa, September 1985, Table 15, pp. 36–37 (Catalogue 81–204 Annual).

Table 8b
UNDERGRADUATE UNIVERSITY ENROLMENT BY
REGISTRATION STATUS AND SEX:
CANADA AND PROVINCES, 1983–1984

	Full-Time				
	Men	Women	Total	Men	Women
	Number			Percentage	
Newfoundland	3,699	3,710	7,409	49.9	50.1
Prince Edward Island	802	874	1,676	47.9	52.1
Nova Scotia	10 648	10 001	20,649	51.6	48.4
New Brunswick	7 134	6 326	13,460	53.0	47.0
Québec	46 888	40 664	87,552	53.6	46.4
Ontario	85 289	77 077	162,366	52.5	47.5
Manitoba	9 801	8 441	18,242	53.7	46.3
Saskatchewan	9 522	8 576	18,098	52.6	47.4
Alberta	18 421	17 249	35,670	51.6	48.4
British Columbia	16 796	15 431	32,227	52.1	47.9
Canada	209,000	188,349	397,349	52.6	47.4
	Part-Time				
Newfoundland	1,342	2,389	3,731	36.0	64.0
Prince Edward Island	241	468	709	34.0	66.0
Nova Scotia	2,225	3,674	5,899	37.7	62.3
New Brunswick	1,495	2,820	4,315	34.6	65.4
Québec	39,234	56,342	95,576	41.1	58.9
Ontario	33,652	52,226	85,878	39.2	60.8
Manitoba	5,129	7,804	12,933	39.7	60.3
Saskatchewan	3,007	5,161	8,168	36.8	63.2
Alberta	5,321	8,507	13,828	38.5	61.5
British Columbia	5,656	8,121	13,777	41.1	58.9
Canada	97,302	147,512	244,814	39.7	60.3

Source: Statistics Canada, Ottawa, *Advance Statistics of Education.* Ottawa, September
1985, Table 8–9, pp. 25–26 (Catalogue 81–220 Annual).

When the results are analyzed, certain differences among the provinces emerge. Full-time "adult students" are found more commonly in some provinces (British Columbia, Alberta, Saskatchewan and Québec) than in others. Moreover, the presence of "traditional" students (under 25 years) in part-time enrolment is more pronounced in Manitoba and British Columbia than elsewhere.

Very few "adult students" over 40 are enrolled full-time. In nine out of ten cases, the bulk of the full-time adult students falls in the 25–39 age group. It should be noted, however, that people aged 40 and over are much more represented among part-time students.

b) by Sex

At the undergraduate level, women slightly outnumber men in all provinces. This situation is primarily due to the considerably higher proportion of women enrolled in part-time studies. In Canada, women account for 60 % of the part-time enrolment at the undergraduate level, and men for 40 % (see Table 8b).

On the other hand, the proportion of men among full-time students is somewhat higher than that of women in all provinces except Prince Edward Island and Newfoundland, although this difference is slight. It thus appears that, at the undergraduate level, the breakthrough achieved by women over the last two decades has affected the entire university system.

c) by Field of Study

The various disciplines are not all equally accessible to part-time students. Table 8c shows that in agriculture and biology, engineering and applied sciences, part-time students are far fewer than elsewhere. On the other hand, part-time students are heavily represented in the fields of education and social sciences.

However, even in areas where greater access has been encouraged, there are considerable disparities among the provinces, and some "open" fields of study are still not very accessible in certain regions.

3. Other Variables Related to Type of Attendance

Only partial data are available for the other variables considered below. We will refer to these variables briefly, in order to bring out certain factors or hypotheses which could be useful in connection with this report.

a) Social Origin

Generally speaking, a particular kind of selective or "elitist" character is attributed to the higher education system. Moreover, research studies and surveys done in Canada tend to demonstrate that a part-time program of study promotes greater equality of opportunity at the university level. The social origin of part-time students is more varied.

In this regard, a research study carried out in Québec for a commission of inquiry dealing with the university system drew the following conclusions:

> "On the whole, part-time students are recruited from more modest social backgrounds. In half of the cases, the father has a white-collar or blue-collar position. They are less often sons or daughters of people at the executive, middle management or professional levels than are full-time students." (Dandurand, 1979:27)

b) Paid Employment

Using an extensive sample of students enrolled in all Québec universities in the fall of 1978, this same study analysed their living conditions, including their concurrent involvment in the labour market:

> "At first glance, the proportion of university students declaring that they held a paid job during the school year appears to be relatively high: 48.8 %. However, this relatively high proportion can be explained largely by the increasingly greater presence of part-time students on campus. In fact, this latter group which makes up

Table 8c
UNDERGRADUATE UNIVERSITY ENROLMENT BY FIELD OF STUDY AND REGISTRATION STATUS: CANADA AND PROVINCES, 1983–1984

Field of Study		Newfoundland	Prince Edward Island	Nova Scotia	New Brunswick	Québec	Ontario	Manitoba	Saskatchewan	Alberta	British Columbia	Canada
Education	(1)	1,368	226	1,423	2,269	22,653	17,684	3,497	4,873	7,447	6,013	67,453
	(2)	53.8	55.3	80.9	84.4	41.3	57.3	63.9	69.6	89.7	66.0	58.8
	(3)	46.2	44.7	19.1	15.6	58.7	42.7	36.1	30.4	10.3	34.0	41.2
Fine/Applied Arts	(1)	36	29	783	297	7,094	6,803	935	578	1,229	1,509	19,293
	(2)	100.0	75.9	89.7	99.3	57.1	81.0	66.7	79.4	85.8	74.0	71.9
	(3)	—	24.1	10.3	0.7	42.9	19.0	33.3	20.6	14.2	26.0	28.1
Humanities	(1)	722	124	1,550	776	13,426	16,371	1,511	1,472	1,531	2,549	40,032
	(2)	67.7	86.3	88.9	90.5	56.4	72.5	59.4	87.9	83.6	69.2	68.3
	(3)	32.3	13.7	11.1	9.5	43.6	27.5	40.6	12.1	16.4	30.8	31.7
Social Sciences	(1)	1,739	851	7,463	4,884	63,457	62,135	6,187	6,849	9,007	9,393	171,965
	(2)	79.4	76.1	82.8	83.3	47.2	73.8	64.3	66.1	72.5	75.0	64.0
	(3)	20.6	23.9	17.2	16.7	52.8	26.2	35.7	33.9	27.5	25.0	36.0
Agriculture/ Biological Sciences	(1)	460	97	1,459	526	5,165	9,212	1,788	2,132	1,584	1,887	24,310
	(2)	91.7	96.9	96.1	99.0	85.8	91.8	82.4	94.8	96.0	88.3	90.5
	(3)	8.3	3.1	3.9	1.0	14.2	8.2	17.6	5.2	4.0	11.7	9.5
Engineering/ Applied Sciences	(1)	600	138	1,864	1,943	13,235	19,515	1,327	1,321	3,640	2,803	46,386
	(2)	70.5	97.1	96.7	97.5	84.5	93.2	93.6	94.2	98.3	93.9	91.3
	(3)	29.5	2.9	3.3	2.5	15.5	6.8	6.4	5.8	1.7	6.1	8.7
Health Professions	(1)	575	—	1,520	601	11,155	8,489	1,231	1,128	2,923	1,953	29,575
	(2)	80.9	—	93.4	72.7	62.7	89.7	84.2	91.7	87.4	89.3	78.8
	(3)	19.1	—	6.6	27.3	37.3	10.3	15.8	8.3	12.6	10.7	21.2
Mathematics/ Physical Sciences	(1)	998	26	1,588	1,242	14,623	14,987	1,354	1,863	2,253	1,174	41,108
	(2)	91.6	100.0	92.5	97.3	45.1	84.6	84.0	83.0	91.9	78.2	72.4
	(3)	8.4	—	7.5	2.7	54.9	15.4	16.0	17.0	8.1	21.8	28.6

Other	(1)	4,642	894	8,898	5,237	32,320	93,048	13,323	6,050	19,892	17,729	202,033
	(2)	54.8	58.2	57.9	46.2	22.9	45.2	42.2	42.6	52.3	59.8	44.2
	(3)	45.2	41.8	42.1	53.8	77.1	54.8	57.8	57.4	47.7	40.2	55.8
Total	(1)	11,140	2,385	26,548	17,775	183,128	248,244	31,153	26,266	49,506	46,010	642,155
	(2)	66.5	70.3	77.8	75.7	47.8	65.4	58.5	68.9	72.1	70.1	61.9
	(3)	33.5	29.7	22.2	24.3	52.2	34.6	41.5	31.1	27.9	29.9	38.1

(1) Total enrolment in the field of study.
(2) Percentage of full-time enrolment.
(3) Percentage of part-time enrolment.

Source: This table was prepared on the basis of information obtained from: Statistics Canada, Ottawa, *Universities: Enrolment and Degrees.* Ottawa, September 1985, Table 1, pp. 2 and 3 (Catalogue 81–204 Annual).

close to 30 % of the population surveyed, represents a higher percentage of students holding jobs (89 %). In addition, this same category of student has the largest concentration of students holding a full-time job. As for full-time students, they represent a smaller proportion (33.2 %) of job-holders with the jobs usually being held on a part-time basis in such cases. Of the total number of full-time students, there were only 6.1 % holding full-time paid jobs." (Dandurand, 1979:114—115)

Table 9

**EMPLOYMENT PROFILE OF UNIVERSITY STUDENTS AT ALL LEVELS
BY REGISTRATION STATUS, QUÉBEC, 1978**

Program of Study	Paid Employment				
	None	Full-time		Part-time	Total
Full-time	66.9	6.0	33.1 %	27.1	100 %
Part-time	10.9	78.4	89.1 %	10.7	100 %
Total	51.3	51.3	48.7 %	22.6	100 %

Source: Dandurand, Pierre; Fournier, Marcel. *Conditions de vie de la population universitaire.* Montréal, Université de Montréal, mai 1979, Tableau 64, p. 115.

c) *Other Variables*

Other variables (overall annual income, marital status, place of residence, etc.) also tend to confirm the existence of well-known differences between the full-time student, who fits the traditional model of an "average" student (single, financially dependent, living with one's parents or sharing an apartment with others), and the part-time student (married, wage-earner, living in one's own house, etc.).

C. POLICIES AND PRACTICES OF HIGHER EDUCATION INSTITUTIONS CONCERNING ADULT STUDENTS

1. Admission Requirements

Generally speaking, students are admitted to university upon obtaining a secondary school leaving certificate or upon completion of 12 years of school (13 in Québec and Ontario). However:

> "Most universities are flexible about admitting to first degree programs, usually those in arts and science, persons with unconventional patterns of previous schooling, provided that they have been out of school for a number of years and can show promise of success in university. The most common requirement for this kind of "mature matriculation" is that applicants be at least 21 years of age and have been away from full-time schooling for two or more years. They may be asked to take some tests and to provide letters of reference, and, if they are admitted, it is likely to be on probation. . . . And some universities waive normal admission requirements for senior citizens." (AUCC, 1982:v)

152

According to a Canadian report submitted to UNESCO for a survey on innovations in education (UNESCO, 1980), 34 universities recognized "mature student" status for purposes of admission at that time. Moreover, a number of universities offer remedial courses (usually of one-year duration) to prepare for university entrance those adults who have not completed their secondary schooling.

Nevertheless, despite slow but sustained progress over the past few years, much remains to be done to facilitate university access for adults who do not meet the usual admission requirements. Although this category of adults now finds it easier to enrol in so-called "continuing education" courses, there are still many instances where they have difficulty gaining admission to degree programs as "regular" students.

It should be noted, however, that universities have developed programs to facilitate access by groups not normally served by a university. For example, undergraduate programs have been set up for native people in Alberta (Morning Star Program at the University of Alberta and the University of Calgary's Outreach Program), in Saskatchewan (the Saskatchewan Indian Federated College at the University of Regina (16)), and in Manitoba (programs designed mainly for Indian students attending Brandon University, and the Inter-Universities North program where three universities work together to offer credit courses north of the 53rd parallel).

Institutions providing instruction at a distance (educational television or communications networks such as the Knowledge Network in British Columbia, ACCESS in Alberta, TVOntario and Radio-Québec) or universities providing remote teaching like the Open Learning Institute in British Columbia, Athabasca University in Alberta, and Télé-université in Québec), apply very flexible admission rules to the activities they have developed. These rules ensure broader access to higher education and to university degrees.

2. Evaluation Options

Even full-time students take a long time (3 to 5 years depending on their discipline) to obtain a first university degree. It is therefore not surprising that adults who can at most manage part-time studies would be daunted by the magnitude of the task they have undertaken. Intermediate forms of recognition such as diplomas and certificates have been introduced to encourage part-time students, and to enable them to mark off milestones in their educational development.

In disciplines where part-time studies are possible, the student can accumulate credits for a certificate (usually a 30-credit program) or for a diploma (usually a 60-credit program).

In the last few years, increasing attention has been paid to the issue of recognition of experience (whether academic and practical) and, hence, the possible transfer of credits. This is an crucial, complex issue.

In recent years, task forces and commissions of inquiry have analyzed the relationship between education and work (17) and have demonstrated the vital importance of this relationship. Recognition of experience and transfer of credits are, in principle, possible. In practice, however, each case must be pleaded on an individual basis, and the student must depend upon the goodwill of the institution concerned.

According to the report of the Commission of Inquiry on Educational Leave and Productivity, adults are often obliged to take subjects they have already mastered, "because the appropriate tests and credit systems do not exist" (1979:112). The absence of clearly established and accepted standards for recognizing experience or diplomas sometimes results in high social and economic costs. As the Skill Development Leave Task Force put it:

> "A student who has completed three years of study in a four-year educational program does not have a formal credential. If this student moves to another province and wishes to complete his or her studies, it is often necessary to start over near the beginning. Not only is the human loss enormous but so is the public funding wasted when students are not able to readily transfer credits between and among Canadian educational institutions and provinces.
> "On the other hand, inter-provincial standards, modular recognition, competency-based testing, credit for previous learning and experiense, self-paced, career-accelerated programs, and the recording of learning involvement through the use of the time-based, non-credit Continuing Education Unit (CEU) are being used in a limited way." (Skill Development Leave Task Force, 1983; I:33)

Institutions offering instruction at a distance are doing pioneer work in this area, because of their very nature, and because of the kind of relationship they maintain with "traditional" universities. For example, the Open Learning Institute in British Columbia recognizes up to 75 % of university courses taken in other institutions, and Alberta's Athabasca University will grant its general bachelor's degree after a few courses (or even no courses) have been taken, provided that the student's record warrants it.

3. Attendance Options

In section A.1(d) we discussed the various forms of attendance that characterize regular programs in so-called "traditional" universities. In this section, we shall briefly examine attendance options at three "non-traditional" universities designed to provide instruction at a distance. Other institutions involved in other educational activities might have proved just as interesting, but I decided to concentrate on these three institutions because of their potential for innovation and their permanent status (18).

a) Athabasca University (Alberta)

Athabasca University, which was established in 1970, is modelled on Great Britain's Open University. It offers home study courses, without a teacher, for adults who wish to obtain a first degree. Courses are offered on a continuous basis, and students can begin their studies at any time during the year.

Athabasca has no teaching staff in the traditional sense of the word, and students learn through multi-media materials. Most Athabasca courses use materials from Great Britain's Open University, the University of Mid-America, and the Coastline Community College. The telephone is extensively used to maintain contacts between students and tutors (Peterson, 1982:20).

Television and other audio-visual forms are also used and, in some local communities, courses are given in class format. The various centres are linked up with one another by means of the technologies employed. This ensures greater interaction among students, and between students and monitors.

b) *Télé-université (Québec)*

The Télé-université was founded in 1972. Depending on the field of study, it offers degrees or certificates in mathematics, French, and sociology. It operates on a semester system and also offers summer courses.

There is no permanent teaching staff. Study groups are assisted by part-time group leaders who are not professors. As a rule, these leaders come from the same milieu as the students. Their role is to facilitate learning. In some cases, discussion groups are regularly used and, in others, instruction is based mainly on work done at home.

In addition to discussion groups, various methods and means are used to facilitate the learning process: television, video-cassettes, course texts.

c) *Open Learning Institute (British Columbia)* (19)

This university was founded in 1978. One of its objectives is to offer adults an undergraduate degree in arts and sciences. The fields of study are the following: economy, history, psychology, English, sociology, geography, mathematics, and biology. The university operates on a trimester system (September, January and May).

Seven regional centres have been set up to provide student counselling services. A library service which takes telephone orders is also available. The Staff consists of some 300 employees, 200 of whom are hired on a contract basis as tutors or course writers. The university-level courses are revised and reviewed by recognized university authorities.

A tutor is provided for each course. Telephone and mail contacts are available. One hundred and twenty credits (i.e., 40 courses at three credits each) are required for a degree.

Though the Institute's main purpose is similar to that of Athabasca University and the Télé-université, it has a broader mandate. In addition to university courses, it must also provide technical and vocational training in different trades as well as basic schooling up to grade 12.

4. *Availability of Information Concerning First Degree Programs* (20)

"The universities and colleges use many media to inform prospective students of their programs of study, facilities, costs, and available aid. They publish calendars, catalogues, *annuaires* or brochures which are normally available free of charge. They

155

produce colourful leaflets; they advertise in the daily press and on radio and television.

These publications of individual institutions are supplemented, in most provinces, by booklets outlining the offerings of all institutions of post-secondary education in the province, and information for the whole of Canada is provided in periodical publications of the Association of Universities and Colleges of Canada, the Canadian Association for University Continuing Education . . .

The Canada Employment and Immigration Commission publishes a guide to college and university programs and also information on careers and employment conditions. Use of computerbased information systems for student guidance is becoming more common."

5. Counselling and Guidance Services in First Degree Programs

Besides the information that they give out, universities offer guidance and counselling services. Moreover, in certain provinces, notably Alberta (consortia) and Saskatchewan (community colleges), public networks of "education brokers" have been established.

In Saskatchewan, a network of community colleges was created in 1973 to provide decentralized education services, from basic education to the university level, to adults across the province. The main purpose of the community college is to coordinate educational services to meet the needs of adults for basic schooling, vocational training or university education. The 16 community colleges are supported by a network of more than 300 advisory committees (made up of voluntereers), which determine the educational needs of the population.

These colleges have no campuses and no teaching staff. Where possible, they use existing institutions (universities and other institutions). The community college only organizes required activities where identified needs cannot be met by existing institutions.

In Alberta, consortia were set up in 1980 to provide the adult population with the required services in terms of post-secondary credit courses. At the present time, there are five consortia made up of post-secondary institutions. Each consortium is assisted by a regional advisory committee (made up of volunteers). The consortium must identify educational needs and ensure an appropriate response. The consortia have close ties with the further education councils, which are responsible for the provision of non-credit instruction.

In addition, Alberta has established a network of professional guidance centres offering individual or group counselling, aptitude and interest tests, as well as reference services on educational opportunities and student aid.

6. Placement Services in First Degree Programs

The Canada Employment and immigration Commission administers campus employment centres for more than 80 universites and colleges in Canada. Each year, these centres assist more than 100,000 students at the post-secondary level.

D. FINANCIAL PROVISIONS: MODES OF FINANCING FOR MATURE STUDENTS

1. *Loans and Bursaries*

Diagram 2 gives a description of the different student aid programs (full-time and part-time) available in the provinces and the territories in 1980—81 (21).

Since the introduction of amendments to the Student Aid Act, in 1983, one section of the Canada Student Loans program is applicable to persons who are receiving a part-time education. Under these provisions:

"Guaranteed loans to needy part-time students to helt cover the cost of tuition fees, books, learning materials, transportation and related expenses.
The Part-Time Plan limits borrowing to an outstanding principal to $2,500 at any one time. Repayment under the Part-Time Plan would start one month after the issuance of the loan, with 24 months to repay individual loans."

The conditions of eligibility are the following:
"Must be a Canadian citizen or permanent resident:
- attending (or planning to attend) a designated postsecondary institution
- a resident of a province that issues loans under the Canada Student Loans Program (all provinces and territories other than Quebec)
- have a gross family income of no more than specified in the following table
- not be in default on previous part-time or full-time Canada Student Loans
- taking between 20 % and 59 % of a full course load."

Table 10a
INCOME CEILINGS FOR PART-TIME STUDENT LOANS

	Single Student	*Married Students — Dependents*					
		1	2	3	4	5	6
Maximum Income							
($)	24,200	26.900	29,700	32,400	35,200	37,900	40,700

Source: Secretary of State, 1983a:20—21)

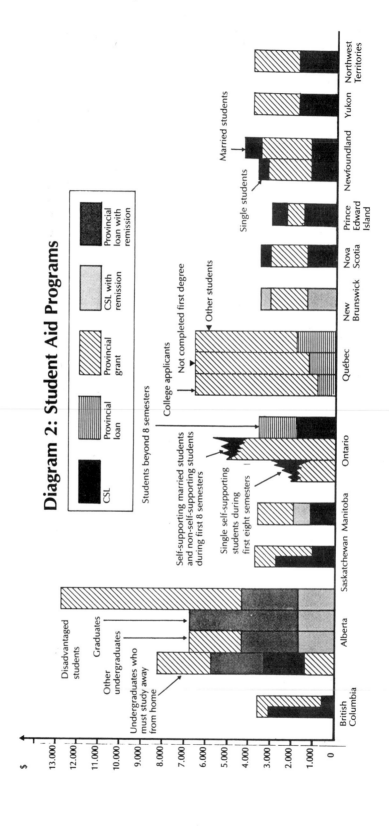

Diagram 2: Student Aid Programs

158

Description of main Programs, 1980–81

British Columbia: First $600 of need is CSL, remaining need to $3000 is half grant, half CSL. Additional to $3500 is grant. Also a work-study component.

Alberta: 1. For non-self-supporting undergraduate students who must live away from home: of the first $5700 of need $1400 is a grant and the remainder is CSLP and provincial loan with remission. The remaining need to $8200 is a grant.

2. Other undergraduate students first $1800 is CSL with remission, next $2500 is provincial loan with remission, remaining need to $6800 is a grant.

3. Graduate students and students in professional fields: first $1800 of need is CSL with remission, remaining need to $6800 is provincial loan with remission.

4. For disadvantaged students the first $4300 of need is (depending on circumstances) CSL and provincial loans with remission. Remaining need to $12.800 is a grant.

Saskatchewan: First $1000 of need is CSL, next $1600 of need is half grant and half CSL, remaining need to $3600 is grant.

Manitoba: First $930 of need is CSL, next $870 of need is CSL with remission, remaining need to $3600 is grant. Maximum remission is $870 which reduces grant maximum by $870.

Ontario: 1. Single self-supporting students in first eight semesters: all need up to $1000/semester is a grant CSL for those who do not meet strict grant criteria.

2. Other students in first eight semesters: all need up to $2500/semester is a grant CSL for those who do not meet strict grant criteria.

3. Students not in the first eight semesters: first $1800 of need is CSL, remaining need to $3600 is provincial loan.

Québec: 1. College applicants: first $810 of need is provincial loan, remaining need to $6500 is a grant.

2. First degree not complete: first $1140 of need is provincial loan, remaining need to $6500 is a grant.

3. Other students: first $1625 of need is a provincial loan, remaining need to $6500 is a grant.

New Brunswick: First $1400 of need is CSL with remission, next $1700 of need is grant, remaining need to $3500 is CSL with remission. Maximum remission is $2250.

Nova Scotia: First $1400 of need is CSL, next $1700 of need is a grant, remaining need to $3500 is CSL.

Prince Edward Island: First $1400 of need is CSL, next $1000 of need is a grant, remaining need to $2800 is CSL.

Newfoundland: 1. Single students: first $1150 of need is CSL, next $2000 of need is a grant, remaining need to $3600 is CSL.

2. Married students: first $1150 of need is CSL, next $2500 of need is a grant, remaining need to $4300 is CSL.

Yukon: First $1800 of need is CSL and there is a separately administered grant to $2100, that is, the student can apply to both.

Northwest Territories: First $1800 of need is CSL and a separately administered bursary to $2000 and a travel and tuition grant.

Source: Based on Council of Ministers of Education, Canada, Toronto – Secretary of State, Ottawa. *Report of the Federal-Provincial Task Force on Student Assistance.* Toronto-Ottawa. 1981.

With regard to provincial programs, we know that four provinces (British Columbia, Alberta, Ontario and Québec) offer limited bursaries to part-time students. In actual fact, assistance programs for part-time studies (both the federal program and the provincial programs mentioned above) are very limited, and could not be considered as a motivating factor in encouraging the adult population to return to school. As noted by the Skill Development Leave Task Force:

"Part-time adult learners are often excluded from financial support and, when there is support, it is based on the maintenance requirements for young people." (Skill Development Leave Task Force, 1983,II:11)

As for loan and bursary programs, this point of view is just as valid in terms of the support provided to full-time students:

"An adult student who would return to school full time must suffer a substantial drop in income. Post-secondary financial support is geared to the financial needs of young family dependents. The staff of the Commission estimated that an adult man with a working wife, two children and a family income of $200,000 per annum would suffer a minimum 40 per cent to 50 per cent drop in family income if he returned to school full time even if he was able to attract the normal amount of current student support." (Commission of Inquiry on Educational Leave and Productivity, 1979:101)

The loan and bursary programs set up by governments are designed as support for studies. No attempt is made here to overcome inequality of access by increasing the participation of young people or adults from a modest background.

The Federal-Provincial Task Force on Student Assistance made the following statement in this regard:

"Student aid programs are necessary but are not sufficient in our society's attempt to reduce those barriers to postsecondary education arising from the socio-economic position of the individual's family. While student aid is a necessary and important source of financing for those who do decide to participate, direct financial considerations are not the major factor in most participation decisions. Major increases in expenditure on student aid would result in only small increases in the participation of students from lower income families." (Federal-Provincial Task Force on Student Assistance, 1981:104)

According to this task force, we should also refrain, in the future, from defining these programs as support measures for policies designed to give adults greater access to education:

"The Task Force felt that, in future, aid programs should not be viewed as powerful vehicles for achieving manpower goals, rather, . . . more coordination with man-power-related programs would be desirable." (Federal-Provincial Task Force on Student Assistance, 1981:151)

We do not have any data that would enable us to determine what proportion of loan and bursary program costs is attribuable to adults (part-time students or students 25 years and over). Part-time student loans (under CSLP) are a new initiative. However, we do know that, for 1980–81, the two levels of government contributed $315 million to student aid at the post-secondary level; 41 % of these funds came from the federal government and 59 % from the provinces.

2. Scholarships

The Federal-Provincial Task Force on Student Assistance has tried to assess the importance of this type of bursary in the financing of postsecondary education for the under − 35 age group.

> "About 15–20 % of students received scholarships worth over $300 (about half receiving a scholarship in only one year). The survey indicates no major decline in the percentage of students receiving such scholarships since 1965. The data, however, refer to scholarships from all sources, including governments and post-secondary institutions, not only from private sources.
> "Private funding programs do not reach a large percentage of students and they have not usually been based on financial need. The Task Force concluded that the existing practice of not counting the full value of such awards in the means test was likely the only reasonable way to ensure that aid programs were not a disincentive to private funding." (Federal-Provincial Task Force on Student Assistance, 1981:111)

3. The Canada Manpower Training Program (CMTP)

The major public adult education program in Canada is called the Canada Manpower Training Program (CMTP). This program was established through the National Training Act (1982). However, regulations arising from this Act prohibit the Canada Employment and Immigration Commission (which administers the agreements signed with the provinces on behalf of the federal government) from financing activities at the university level.

In a paper prepared at the request of the Skill Development Leave Task Force, the former chairman of the Commission of Inquiry on Educational Leave and Productivity maintained that the CEIC should have sufficient latitude to "buy" training at the university level, and thus be able to influence the universities on behalf of adults. As Roy J. Adams noted, the CEIC has considerable purchasing power in terms of training because it can finance up to 1,820 hours of training for each student that it supports. Moreover, a student working towards a first degree on a full-time basis for four years receives no more than 1,800 hours of instruction in all.

Adults studying full-time in this program are entitled to either training allowances or unemployment insurance benefits. The amounts allocated take into account previous income from former jobs, or family dependents.

> "The Canada Manpower Training Program of Employment and Immigration Canada provides courses to some 175,000 clients annually. Just over half of these are under 25 years of age. Direct income support for these students amounts to $90 million in training allowances and $170 million in unemployment insurance benefits payable under Section 39 of the Unemployment Insurance Act. Some of these students are also eligible for CSLP loans." (Federal-Provincial Task Force on Student Assistance, 1981:152)

161

4. Paid Employment

"Student assistance programs based on need are only one way in which governments and other bodies provide financial assistance to students and their parents. Other programs . . . in their totality, provide more money to students than does student aid based on financial need.

Government financing plays an important role in the most important source of student financing: summer employment. In the summer of 1980, for example, the federal government spent some $120 million and the provinces in total spent another $200 million on summer job creation and placement programs for students (including secondary school students). One of the objectives of summer job creation programs, of course, is to provide resources to allow students to return to school." (Federal-Provincial Task Force on Student Assistance, 1981:151)

In addition, some provincial governments (British Columbia, for example) offer students the opportunity of holding a paid job concurrent with their studies.

5. Tax Exemptions Applicable to Students

According to a global estimate made by the Federal-Provincial Task Force on Student Assistance, tax exemptions claimed by full-time students (either for tuition fees or for living expenses (22)) greatly exceeded $100 million for 1979.

"Qualifying educational programs are programs of not less than three weeks duration where a student must spend at least 10 hours a week on courses or work in the program. In some cases, the program must be at the post-secondary school level.

Although the deductions claimed by students under the Income Tax Act do not represent a direct expenditure by the Government of Canada, they are considered as a tax expenditure because the government foregoes revenues by allowing these deductions for students. This is also true of other tax exemptions that benefit educational institutions or students, for example: non-taxation of up to $500 of scholarship, fellowship or bursary income; exemption from sales tax of certain educational materials bought by educational institutions; and the charitable status designation of many educational institutions allowing supporters to deduct donations from their personal taxable income." (Secretary of State, 1983b:16—17)

We are not in a position to estimate what proportion of these tax exemptions can be attributed to "adult students".

6. Payment of Tuition Fees by Employer

Enterprises frequently provide their employees with tuition aid plans for education or training acitivites undertaken outside of regular working time. Although this type of on—the—job training assistance for employees is rather widespread, relatively few of the employees entitled to tuition aid make use of this option. According to a 1981 Québec-based survey on training in industry, 51 % of enterprises had schemes for reimbursement of their employees' tuition fees. Nevertheless, in enterprises reporting this type of program, the number of recipients amounted to less than 6 per cent. (Paquet, 1982:67)

Table 10 shows that enterprises often made such reimbursements to their

162

employees in connection with courses taken at an educational institution. Moreover, of the 83 % of enterprises reporting reimbursements of this kind, "64.5 % had reimbursed tuition fees for university-level courses, 47.2 % for college-level courses and 22.1 % for secondary-level courses." (Paquet, 1982:79)

Table 10b

PERCENTAGE OF ENTERPRISES HAVING REIMBURSED TUITION FEES BY TYPE OF EDUCATIONAL SERVICE

		Businesses
Type of Educational Service	Number	Per cent[1]
Sector association	65	17.0
Professional or technical association	115	33.4
Private educational establishment	113	32.9
Educational institution	286	83.3

[1]These percentages cannot be added together as more than one answer is possible.
Source: Paquet, Pierre; Doray, Pierre; Bouchard, Pierre. *Sondage sur les pratiques de formation en entreprise.* Québec, Ministère des Communications, 1982, p. 79.

7. Tax Exemptions Applicable to Enterprises

An employer who incurs expenses related to the provision of training opportunities for his or her employees can deduct these as a business expense:

> "to the extent that they are reasonable in the circumstances, no matter whether the training is for the benefit of himself or the employee." (Revenue Canada, 1980:3)

If the training is provided by an educational institution, the employer can deduct the cost of tuition fees paid on behalf of the employee.

8. Educational Leave

Research done for the Commission of Inquiry on Educational Leave and Productivity (23) has shown that educational leave is not commonly granted by businesses in Canada. Neither is there a national paid educational leave program to ensure access to university education for adults (or at least adults from a rather modest socio-economic background). Less than 10 % of enterprises reported this type of training assistance and, in 1978, leave-takers represented a minimal percentage of the employees working for the enterprises surveyed. The same survey revealed that nine leave-takers out of ten were from the public sector. (Commission of Inquiry on Educational Leave and Productivity, 1979:170−171)

Since then, two other studies have confirmed the conclusions reached by the Commission. Fortunately, these two studies used the same definition of (long-term) educational leave as the Commission had used (full-time studies for a minimum of three months).

163

The most recent of these two studies, which was undertaken for the Skill Development Leave Task Force and Covered the period of 1982, showed that 9.2 % of enterprises in Canada reported (long-term) educational leave programs. (Social Program Evaluation Group, 1983:24)

The second study, which was done for Québec's Commission on Adult Education, deals with the 1980–81 period. It indicated that 13.5 % of enterprises reported educational leave programs, and that the involvement of the public sector in such activities was much greater (28.1 %) than that of the private sector (7.7 %). (Paquet, 1983:20)

E. ATTITUDES CONCERNING ADULT PARTICIPATION IN FIRST DEGREE PROGRAMS

1. Institutions

In quantitative terms, adults (read part-time students) now occupy a fairly important position in universities, but their real weight in the university system seems more limited than their numbers would justify. The universities are well aware that their traditional clientele (the 18–24 age group) is levelling off. The medium- or long-term survival of the universities depends on ensuring greater access for adults undertaking part-time studies.

However, these new clienteles at times present considerable challenges to the teaching staff:

> "The relationship between the teaching body and these everchanging clienteles which are difficult to forecast is quite different from the traditional one. These new students are both more mature and yet often less immediately capable of handling intellectual work. There are many difficulties involved in compelling them to use proven methods to acquire knowledge. Moreover, this relationship differs from the kind of relationship that would develop with younger students who are less preoccupied with professional and family responsibilities. (Bertrand, 1982:80)

Viewed from the outside, the manner in which the universities are responding to this changing situation gives rise to rather negative reactions. Universities are criticized for their lack of flexibility or even their indifference towards part-time students. The services provided for this category of student are often inadequate (e.g., no services in the evenings or on weekends).

Certain incentive measures are being recommended to encourage the universities to respond to the needs of part-time students. But the expectation is that, in return, the universities will stop acting as if they have "a monopoly in deciding what is appropriate and relevant". (Skill Development Leave Task Force, 1983: vol. I–79)

2. Employers

> "The integration of work and time off as a mechanism for training and upgrading employees' skills is already in place, is proving to be effective, and will become

more prevalent as new technology is introduced to the work place." (Skill Development Leave Task Force, 1983: vol. I—85).

This point of view as reported by the Task Force accurately expresses the position of industry on the question of training and educational leave for workers. It is felt that the private sector is already in a position to respond to needs and that, with anticipated technological change, its efforts will intensify during the years to come.

Employers are therefore opposed to government intervention in this sector through legislative means, and reject the idea of educational leave as a universal right. They also reject the proposal that Canada ratify Convention 140 of the ILO. To put it simply, the government is being asked to look after the unemployed and to let the private sector look after the job training needs of workers. According to the report commissioned by the Skill Development Leave Task Force, it appears that opposition is stronges among the businesses that already offer training programs. The main reason given for their opposition is the desire to concentrate maximum control over training programs in the hands of management.

Another opinion expressed in the section of the Task Force report dealing with the employers' viewpoint sheds more light (of the same kind) on the private sector's position on educational leave:

> "All objections previously raised are still considered valid and any new definition of skill development leave which broadens the interpretation historically taken by industry and thus changes the basis of industrial relations in Canada is opposed by employers." (Skill Development Leave Task Force, 1983: vol. I—85)

3. *Government*

During the last five years, at the federal level, various commissions, task forces, etc. have taken many direct and indirect approaches to the issue of workers' training and adult education. The recommendations go off in several directions, and are sometimes contradictory. One way to summarize the question confronting governments (in particular the federal government in its own jurisdictional sphere) would be as follows: "Should governments wait until workers lose their jobs before intervening or is it possible to develop scenarios allowing certain types of prevention or affirmative action?"

At the provincial level, it seems that a certain number of governments have chosen to cast adult education in a supporting role in relation to economic recovery and manpower policies.

Chapter II
Adults in continuing education programs provided by universities and higher education institutions

A. BACKGROUND: THE ACADEMIC AND NON-ACADEMIC INSTITUTIONS THAT PROVIDE CONTINUING EDUCATION

Adult education in Canada has been aptly described as follows:

> "The overriding feature of Canadian adult education is its diffuseness. There does not exist, in Canada as a whole, a coherent articulated system of adult education. It can best be described as complex, highly decentralized, variably funded, and largely invisible. (Clark, 1982:210)

Because of the diffuse nature of adult education, the statistics relating to what is defined here as "continuing education" will not be as well substantiated as those presented in the first part where one type of institution served as a reference. In the adult education field, we find many entities employing a diversity of methods and formats, but few sources of information.

1. Institutions and Enrolments

a) Institutions

The last twenty years has witnessed a massive expansion in educational opportunities for adults. Current resources for adult learning are many and varied including such diverse providers as public and private schools, labour unions, voluntary organizations, churches, libraries, broadcasting media, museums, and employers who offer courses, workshops, conferences, seminars, and educational publications. Community colleges and universities are the most important providers. In sum, the range of providers is so diverse that it may appear un-coordinated and even confused. (CAAE ICEA, 1982:21)

The following is a look at the main adult education services in Canada.

Colleges and Universities

Since the 1960s, most Canadian jurisdictions have developed systems of community colleges to parallel the university network across the country. Both institutions offer extensive services to adults on both part-time and full-time bases and through both credit and non-credit programs. Atkinson College at York University, for example, offers only part-time credit courses. Other adult-serving institutions include Athabasca University and Télé-université which specialize in distance education.

School Boards

In several provinces, Boards of Education include among their responsibilities the provision of adult education services. Some of the larger urban Boards are among the biggest single providers of adult education in the country. In other provinces, school boards enjoy no competence in the education of adults.

Libraries and Cultural Institutions

Many Canadians would be surprised to learn just how extensive are the adult learning services and opportunities created daily by public libraries, museums and art galleries throughout the country.

Residential Centres

This type of institution offers adult education, usually on a concentrated, intensive basis. They are operated by governments, corporations, voluntary organizations, universites, colleges and churches. Some are profit-making institutions.

Labour Education

The CAAE/ICEA survey suggests that members of unions are more likely than the rest of the population to be learners. Some of this differential may be explained by the extensive learning service unions operate for their more than two million members in Canada. This effort has been supported by governments in recent years, but there are indications that such funding may be threatened.

Gitizens' Groups and Voluntary Organizations
These organizations offer very substantial amounts of adult learning opportunities, but their very nature prevents accurate measurement. In Quebec, for example, many of these groups have joined together under the name of MEPACQ (Popular Education and Community Action Movement of Quebec), in order to make their unique work known and to seek funds.

Educational Media
One of the most powerful forces for learning in our society is television. Governments have recognized this fact and, in five provinces, have created educational television services to enhance the delivery of educational services. Millions of Canadians receive this service. It is distance-free and offers flexible hours for viewing. Some programs are interactive.

Training-on-the-Job, Apprenticeship and In-Service Training
Such opportunities are undertaken by all kinds of employers. Among the leaders are governments and major employers in the private sector. (CAAE-ICEA, 1982:21—22)

We can add to this list professional associations that ensure the competence of their members by means of continuing education programs. According to a recent study, 33 groups reported that they organized training programs for their members in 1979. (Peterson, 1982:83)

b)   Enrolments
What is the estimated participation rate of the adult population in education in Canada? According to recent calculations, the estimated participation rate in adult education at all levels and for all types was 23 % (see Table 11).

As subject to caution as it might be, Table 11 nevertheless offers an order of magnitude for the volume of activities and participation rate in adult education around the years 1976—77 in Canada. The leading role of the public education institutions is clearly apparent.

If we look at the most recent data from a 1983 survey conducted jointly by the Canadian Association for Adult Education (CAAE) and the Institut canadien d'éducation des adultes (ICEA), we see that the provision of training activities is distributed in the following manner in terms of adults who participated in such activities during the last three years: public education institutions provide half of the programs, employers provide about 20 %, unions and voluntary associations 10 %, and other sources the remaining 20 % or so (see Table 12).

What percentage of adults (24) received training and what percentage did not? The CAAE-ICEA 1982 and 1983 surveys provided different estimates of adult involvement in educational activities. A first indicator attempts to determine what percentage of adults took what they considered to be courses at one time or other since the completion of their initial schooling. Excluding those who are not considered adults, the results showed that 43 % of the respondents participated of their initial schooling. In the 1982 survey, these percentages were 34 % and 66 % respectively.

These surveys also helped to establish the percentage of active learners (i.e., adults having taken courses during the last year or the last three years). In

Table 11
CANADA: MAJOR PROGRAMS AND ESTIMATES OF PARTICIPATION

Program or Provider	Estimated Number of Participants	Year	Source
University Continuing Education	574,000	1976—77	Statistics Canada, 1979
University Part-Time	211,700	1977—78	Statistics Canada, 1979
Community Colleges — Continuing Education	450,000	1976—77	Statistics Canada, 1978
Departments of Education — Correspondence Courses	91,000	1976—77	Statistics Canada, 1979
School Boards — Credit and non-credit	639,000	1976—77	Statistics Canada, 1979
Canada Manpower Training Program	280,000	1976—77	CMTP, 1977
Ontario Training in Business and Industry	15,000	1977—78	Statistics Canada, 1979
Registered Apprentices	106,000	1977—78	Adams, 1979
Employer Day Release Training	398,000	1977—78	Adams, 1979
Employer Extended Leave Training	10,000	1977—78	Adams, 1979
Labour Education	227,000	1975	Pearl, 1975 plus author
New Horizons	100,000	1976	Statistics Canada, 1979
Parent Education — Ontario	332,000	1978	Secretary for Social Development, 1979
Total Adult Population			14,869,000
Estimated total participation rate			23 %
Estimated total participation, all programs			3,433,700

Source: Peterson, Richard E., et al. Adult Education and Training in Industrialized Countries. New York, Praeger, 1982, Table 2, p. 25.

1982−83, 20 % of the adult population took courses (in 1981−82 the figure was 18 %). If we look at the last three years, the percentage of active learners climbs to 29 %. It should be noted that we are dealing with all levels of education regardless of how it is provided.

2. *Programs of Study*

When we try to determine the more specific role of various adult education services, we find that some information is available with regard to universities, industry and the labour unions. As for the other services, the data are incomplete, not comparable or quite simply nonexistent. To provide a more complete and substantial picture, we would have had to criss-cross the country and unearth documents buried here and there, without having any assurance as to the reliability of the resulting overview.

a) *In Universities*

Global data on continuing education in Canadian universities were last published by Statistics Canada in 1978. This material covers both non-credit and credit part-time studies (degree, diploma or certificate programs). The data presented here are distributed by province for the years 1976−77 (see Table 13).

Table 12
ROLE OF ADULT EDUCATION PROVIDERS
IN TERMS OF LEARNERS (OVER THE LAST THREE YEARS) IN CANADA

Provider	*Per Cent[1]*
University	17.
Community College/CGEP	22.
School Board	12.
Employer	21.
Union	3.
Voluntary Association[2]	7.
Other	22.

(1) These percentages cannot be added together, as more than one answer is possible.
(2) Based on additional information provided by the CAAE, a supplementary category (Voluntary Association) has been added, thereby reducing the "Other" category from 29 % to 22 %.

Source: CAAE, Toronto. *Paid Educational Leave.* Toronto, April 30, 1983, P. 34.

b) *In Industry*

In the case of firms providing training programs, the importance of work-related training activities is noticeable. On the other hand, enterprises less frequently offer general or social education programs. Different surveys have demonstrated that, as a general rule, enterprises provide short term training.

Table 13

**NUMBER OF STUDENTS IN CREDIT AND NON-CREDIT COURSES:
CANADA AND PROVINCES, 1976–77**

	Part-Time Credit Courses	Non-Credit Courses	Total
	Number		
Newfoundland	5,377	3,595	8,972
Prince Edward Island	2,056	237	2,293
Nova Scotia	11,353	9,259	20,612
New Brunswick	8,212	3,995	12,207
Québec	110,062	37,954	148,016
Ontario	137,289	75,106	212,395
Manitoba	19,997	9,035	29,032
Saskatchewan	12,958	13,032	25,990
Alberta	20,987	40,353	61,340
British Columbia	19,078	34,400	53,478
Canada	347,369	226,966	575,335
	Per Cent		
Newfoundland	*59.9*	*40.1*	
Prince Edward Island	*89.7*	*10.3*	
Nova Scotia	*55.1*	*44.9*	
New Brunswick	*67.3*	*22.7*	
Québec	*74.7*	*25.6*	
Ontario	*64.6*	*35.4*	
Manitoba	*68.9*	*31.1*	
Saskatchewan	*49.9*	*50.1*	
Alberta	*34.2*	*65.8*	
British Columbia	*35.7*	*64.3*	
Canada	*60.5*	*39.5*	

Source: Statistics Canada, Ottawa, *Continuing Education: Universities.* Ottawa, May 1978, Table 2, p. 24 (Catalogue 81–225 Annual), discontinued publication.

This table shows the considerable differences in the distribution of "adult students" enrolled in credit and non-credit courses. Whereas participation in non-credit courses is limited in Prince Edward Island, practically two-thirds of the adult students in Alberta and British Columbia are enrolled in non-credit courses.

c) In Labour Organizations

According to data gathered by the Commission of Inquiry on Educational Leave and Productivity, 25 % of employees in enterprises reporting training programs are covered by agreements with long-term educational leave provision, and 31 % by agreements with short-term educational leave provisions (Clark, 1982:227).

The phenomenon observed in employer-organized training recurs in training provided by labour organizations:

"Resources to mount systematic educational programs were generally available only in the larger (industrial) unions. In 69 per cent of the local unions there proved to be no person assigned a specific responsibility for education. This was the case in three-fourths of the unions not affiliated with the CLC or Quebec's Confederation of National Trade Unions (CNTU). Of 118 national and international unions affiliated with the CLC (25), only 18 had a recognized education department." (Clark, 1982:227)

The main union education centre at the university level is called the Canadian College of Workers. This centre is administered jointly by the Canada Labour Congress (CLC), the University of Montreal and McGill University. Training consists of an eight-week program with courses in economics, labour law, political science, industrial sociology, and the history of the labour movement. The College has been in operation since 1963.

Another establishment, the Atlantic Region Labour Education Centre (ARLEC), is located in Nova Scotia and operates in association with Saint Francis Xavier University.

3. Organization

a) In Universities

Chapter A described "non-traditional" institutions and the various methods developed to meet the educational needs of adults. In particular, the non-credit education sector has been responsible for all kinds of experiments, projects, and activities ranging from cultural activities to community services. These have promoted both individual and community development. However, these particular sectors often represent marginal activities within the university system. Between 1979 and 1984, an inter-university fund in Québec has provided an estimated $½ million to facilitate community and group development initiatives by means of innovative projects combining training, research and provision of required services.

Modern technology, associated with television instruction, has facilitated access to continuing education programs, particularly in regions located at a distance from urban centres or educational institutions. The development of new institutions with an outreach mission and based on volunteer involvement (for example, the Further Education Councils and Consortia in Alberta and the advisory committees linked to community colleges in Saskatchewan) has facilitated the matching of community needs of the clientele and university resources, among others.

b) In Industry

Training in industry mainly takes place during regular working hours (this was the case for 84 % of leave-takers in Québec in 1980–81). This mainly involves off-the-job training activities (rather than on-the-job training).

According to data gathered in Québec, training during working hours is provided either directly by the employer or in association with private agencies.

The public institutions play a secondary role at this level. On the other hand, when training occurs on the employee's time (tuition aid programs), educational institutions (mainly universities) play a major role (Paquet, 1982:76–79)

c) *In Labour Organizations*

Labour education is provided by means of weekend sessions, evening courses and short-term programs (up to a maximum of a week). However, the Canadian College of Workers offers eight-week programs in a residential centre.

Table 14
EXPENDITURES ON NON-CREDIT INSTRUCTION REPORTED BY THE UNIVERSITIES:
CANADA AND PROVINCES, 1981–82

	Amount of Expenses ($000)	*Percentage in Relation to Operating Expenses*
Newfoundland	2,492	2.4
Prince Edward Island	—	—
Nova Scotia	1,535	0.7
New Brunswick	383	0.3
Québec	12,208	0.9
Ontario	16,007	0.9
Manitoba	2,349	1.1
Saskatchewan	3,924	2.0
Alberta	10,017	2.0
British Columbia	9,099	1.8
Canada	58,014	1.2

Source: Statistics Canada, Ottawa. *Financial Statistics of Education, 1981–82.* Ottawa, December 1984, Table 15, pp. 70–71 (Catalogue 81–208 Annual).

The United Automobile Workers (UAW) have also developed a training program for their members using the paid educational leave clauses negotiated in most of their collective agreements. The method used in this case involves staggered time periods. Training takes place over four periods, each lasting a week. Each period is followed by two to three weeks off with studying done at home. The English-speaking program is offered at the UAW training centre in Port Elgin (Ontario), and the French-speaking program is offered in a suburb of Québec City at Laval University's Forestry Centre.

4. *Financing Programs*

a) *In Universities*

Students enrolled in credit courses can benefit from provincial government grants. As a general rule, these amounts are calculated for grant purposes by determining the number of part-time students (3.5 enrolments, for example) that make up a full-time student equivalent.

On the other hand, non-credit education must be self-financed. Of course, since the university infrastructure is already in place, non-credit education has access to certain services and benefits from reduced costs. Nonetheless, the direct costs of such activities are generally borne by the users. In these circumstances, it is difficult to develop some services (such as community services) particularly for groups that have not previously had access to university education before.

We are not in a position to assess what portion of government grants to universities should be attributed to part-time students in credit courses who are not planning to obtain a first university degree. As for non-credit education, Table 14 indicates the expenses reported by each province in this area.

In Section B. 1(1), it was noted that non-credit enrolments were proportionately higher in the western provinces (where this type of enrolment represented the majority of part-time students in 1976−77). If the financial data in Table 14 can be considered reliable, it would seem that this situation still prevailed in 1981−82, since the western provinces reported increased expenditures on non-credit instruction in this period.

b) In Industry

Industrial training activities are for the most part financed directly by employers rather than through public subsidies. It should be noted, however, that companies' expenditures on training (including amounts spent on tuition aid programs) are entirely tax deductible.

As mentioned in section A. 5 (d), there is some doubt as to the reliability of estimates of expenditures by industry on training activities. Researchers who have attempted to calculate these amounts have stated that it is not possible to produce reliable data for this item.

c) In Labour Organizations

Most of the funds used to finance labour education activities come from members' dues. Nevertheless, as mentioned previously, certain unions such as the United Automobile Workers (UAW) have negotiated paid educational leave clauses. Under these agreements, the employer contributes one cent per course hour and per employee to a training fund controlled by the union. Grants are another source of funds:

> "Since 1977−78, the Federal Government of Canada has provided grants to central trade union organizations for the purpose of establishing labour education programs to enable offiers, staff members and potential trade union leaders to acquire a more extensive knowledge of the labour movement and its goals, and the skills necessary to perform their jobs in the trade union movement.'" (Skill Development Leave Task Force, 1983: vol. I−70)

According to information received by Task Force members in May, 1983 from representatives of the Department of Labour (which is responsible for this

174

program), it is anticipated that $16.5 million will be allocated to this program for the next three years. (Skill Development Leave Task Force, 1983: vol. I—130)

5. *Financing Tuition and Living Accommodation Costs*
Generally speaking, part-time students receive little governmental support. Even less support is available for non-credit education and selffinancing is the general rule. In certain cases, workers can be reimbursed by their employers. A number of firms have tuition aid programs of which the main condition is that the course(s) be related to the duties or position of the employee concerned.

Labour education is one of the few forms of continuing education to receive direct government support. However, the level of support is quite limited in comparison to budgets for the education system as a whole.

B. CHARACTERISTICS OF STUDENTS IN CONTINUING EDUCATION PROGRAMS

The information concerning the characteristics of adults in continuing education programs is taken from the two CAAE-ICEA studies already mentioned which survey the field of adult education as a whole. Although, therefore these data do not allow for the identification of adults attending universities, they provide a useful overall picture from which the situation of adult higher education students is not likely to deviate substantially. On the whole, information and precise data on this population are sketchy. Consequently, the information will be provided globally, regardless of the educational services used.

1. *Participation in Continuing Education by Age*
The results of the CAAE-ICEA survey show that in both the learner and active learner categories the participation rate of adults aged 45 years and over is considerably lower than that of the 25—44 age group. The 1983 CAAE-ICEA survey used modified age categories: 18—29 years; 30—49 years; 50 years and over. However, the results of the 1983 survey identify the same trend: the participation rate of learners in the 30—49 age group is 52 %, whereas in the case of adults aged 50 and over it falls to 28 %.

2. *Participation in Continuing Education by Sex*
A comparison of the two surveys does not allow for a consideration of significant differences according to the sex of adult learners.

3. *Participation in Continuing Education by Educational Attainment*
In 1982 as in 1983, the two surveys identify considerable differences according to educational attainment. As the ICEA emphasized in its submission to the Skill Development Leave Task Force:

"Of all the factors affecting participation in adult education, previous educational attainment is undoubtedly the most important. It has, in fact, been clearly demonstrated (with a high degree of correlation) that regardless of sex or age, participation in adult education activities increases in proportion to the level of schooling reached in the formal education system (schools, colleges, universities, etc.). Conversely, the less formal schooling a person has, the fewer are his or her chances of participating in adult education, even though such a person is "theoretically" most in need of such education. As paradoxical as it may seem, this statement of the facts casts doubt on the belief that adult education can be an alternative for people who want to catch up academically or professionally, and thereby improve their chances in the labour market." (ICEA, 1983:5−6)

4. *Participation in Continuing Education by Income*
For both learners and active learners, the two CAAE-ICEA surveys demonstrate that the participation rates increase with income. As in the case of educational attainment, the differences are quite significant.

5. *Participation in Continuing Education by Occupation*
Educational access varies appreciably according to socio-professional status, and professionals and technicians are in a much more favourable situation. Office employees also enjoy greater access. On the other hand, unskilled workers, the unemployed and housewives are in a less favourable position.

The CAAE-ICEA surveys of participation levels in adult education thus tend to show that all adults do not have equality of access. Given the lack of support for part-time students, the absence of an educational leave policy which would facilitate return to school, and the fact that continuing education at the university level is a self-financing proposition, one can assume that the situation prevailing in the adult education sector as a whole is identical to what we find in the universities.

CONCLUSION

The data available at the present time do not permit a more in-depth exploration of what has been identified here as university continuing education. As we mentioned at the beginning, the decision to distinguish between adults attending university degree programs and other adult education activities tends to reinforce a dichotomy which closely corresponds to reality as it exists in the university milieu. At the same time, the decision contradicts the concept and the philosophy of continuing education.

Nevertheless, it appears that educational thinkers are not the only ones hoping that the university system will adapt to a changing society. The institutional obstacles are well known. There is much to be done to overcome the resistance of some university people towards changes which are being called for on all sides. However, all alone, the universities are not capable of reversing the situation.

It is evident that there is equally strong resistance from other quarters. In many cases, consensus has yet to be established, and the positions of the various partners are quite far apart. Moreover, the distribution of powers in Canada is such that, with education being the responsibility of the provinces, the puzzle becomes even more complex. On the whole, it is fair to say that "Alice's question in Wonderland, 'Cheshire-Puss, would you tell me, please, which way I ought to go from here?' answered as usual by 'That depends a good deal on where you want to get to', fits the current Canadian situation.

List of Abbreviations

AUCC: Association of Universities and Colleges of Canada. Ottawa
CAAE: Canadian Association of Adult Education. Toronto
CEIC: Canada Employment and Immigration Commission. Ottawa
CMEC: Council of Ministers of Education, Canada. Toronto
CSLP: Canada Student Loans Program
ICEA: Institut canadien d'éducation des adultes. Montréal

Notes and References

1 In 1983−84, 70 of these institutions were located in Québec, 16 in British Columbia, 8 in Alberta, and 1 Saskatchewan (Statistics Canada, 1985b:74−75). In 1983−84, the total full-time enrolment in university transfer programs had reached 89, 196, i.e., 75,743 in Québec, 10,002 in British Columbia, 3,411 in Alberta and 40 in Saskatchewan. (Statistics Canada, 1985a:24)

2 The great majority of universities in the ten provinces are members of this association. At the national level, the Association represents one of the major sources of information, dialogue and analysis on the university system in Canada. Seventy institutions belong to the AUCC, and 59 of these have the power to grant degrees. Twelve of the latter group, however, hold this power in abeyance because of their institutional link with another university.

3 Queen's University in Ontario.

4 According to the provisional statistics currently available, there were 741,890 students enrolled in Canadian universities in 1985−86 (651,360 at the undergraduate level and 90,530 at the graduate level). (Statistics Canada, 1985a:25−26)

5 Newfoundland has now added a 12th school year before university entrance. In the future, this change will no doubt bring Newfoundland statistics more in line with those of the other provinces.

6 It should be noted that the definition of a part-time student is broader in Québec than in the other provinces (up to 80 % of a full-time student's workload as opposed to 60 %). Moreover, Québec is the only province where a *considerable* number of full-time students are enrolled in university transfer courses (75,743 young Québecers were in this situation in 1983−84). In the statistics presented in this report, the number of full-time students attending Québec universities has consequently been reduced by this number.

7 This section consists of extracts drawn from the *Directory of Canadian Universities 1982−1983*, published by the AUCC (pp. i−iii).

8 A calender of university correspondence courses is published each year by the Canadian Association for University Continuing Education (CAUCE).

9 The details presented in this section are taken from the *Report of the Federal-Provincial Task Force on Student Assistance.* Mention is made of *twelve* programs, which is a reference to the ten provinces and the two territories (the Yukon and the Northwest Territories). These two territories do not have any universities, but they do provide a postsecondary student aid program.

10 The information presented in this section is taken from the *Report of the Federal-Provincial Task Force on Student Assistance*, pp. 151–152.

11 The figure of 11.7 % represents about 2.2 million people.

12 The figure of 5.8 % represents about 1.1 million people.

13 The attendance rates presented here reflect the number of students aged 25 and over in relation to the total population aged 25 and over.

14 The rate of 1.6 % represents about 220,000 people.

15 The rate of 5.8 % represents a little more than 800,000 people.

16 This unique university-level institution is entirely controlled by Indians. It provides education for Indians who are called upon to perform professional work in a variety of fields (the arts, education, management and administration, social work, guidance counselling, etc.).

17 Let us mention, for example, reports submitted by the following: the Commission of Inquiry on Educational Leave and Productivity (Ottawa, 1979), Commission d'étude sur la formation des adultes (Québec, 1982), Skill Development Leave Task Force (Ottawa, 1983), and the National Advisory Panel on Skill Development Leave (Ottawa, 1984).

18 All three institutions have now moved beyond the experimental stage.

19 Most of the information presented in this section is taken from the following article: Kaufman, David; Sweet, Robert. "Increased Educational Opportunity for Adults: A Canadian Example", *Higher Education*, 8(3), July–September 1983, pp. 15–25.

20 The information contained in this section is taken from the following publication: Council of Ministers of Education, Canada. *Aspects of Postsecondary Education in Canada.* Toronto, 1981, p. 13.

21 The maximum amounts mentioned here are applicable to 1980–81. These amounts may have been readjusted in the last few years, but the program structure and the size of financial aid remain the same.

22 The full-time student is entitled to deduct from his income an amount of $50 per month of full-time studies.

23 This three-member commission was chaired by a university professor. The other two members were a representative of the business community and a representative of labour.

24 "The Institut and the Association define 'adult' to include all persons beyond the compulsory school attendance age in each Canadian juristdiction who have interrupted their continuous attendance at an educational institution for a significant period of labour force participation or other activities." (CAAE-ICEA, 1982:4)

25 About two-thirds of unionized workers across Canada belong to the Canadian Labour Congress.

Bibliography

Adams, Roy J. *Skill Development for Working Canadians — Toward a National Strategy.* Hamilton, McMaster University, March 1983.

Advanced Education and Manpower (Alberta). *It's About Time . . . To Start Thinking About Your Future.* Edmonton, 1983.

Anisef, Paul. "Accessibility Barriers to Higher Education in Canada and Other Countries with Recommendations for Enhancing Accessibility in the Eighties" in Council of Ministers of Education, Canada, *Postsecondary Education Issues in the 1980s.* CMEC, Toronto, 1983, pp. 17—58.

Anisef, Paul; Okihiro, Norman R.; James, Carl. *Losers and Winners: The Pursuit of Equality and Social Justice in Higher Education.* Toronto, Butterworths, 1982.

Association of Universities and Colleges of Canada. *Compendium of University Statistics.* Ottawa, AUCC, 1983.

Association of Universities and Colleges of Canada, Ottawa. *Directory of Canadian Universities 1982—1983.* Ottawa, 1982.

Belanger, R.; Lynd, D.; Mouelhi, M. *Part-Time Degree Students: Tomorrow's Majority?* Ottawa, Statistics Canada, November 1982. (Catalogue 81—573).

Bertrand, Marie-Andrée. "To whom is Postsecondary Education Available? in Council of Ministers of Education, Canada, *Postsecondary Education Issues in the 1980s.* Toronto, CMEC, 1983, pp. 59—91.

Betcherman, Gordon. *Meeting Skill Requirements: Report of the Human Resources Survey.* Ottawa, Economic Council of Canada, 1982.

Bourgeault, Guy, et al. *Les practiques d'éducation permanente au Québec et les universités.* Montréal, Université de Montréal, 1983.

Canadian Association for Adult Education, Toronto. *Paid Educational Leave.* Toronto, CAAE, April 1983.

Canadian Association for Adult Education, — Institut canadien d'éducation des adultes. *From the Adult's Point of View.* CAAE-ICEA, 1982.

Cassidy, Franck. *Continuing Education Policy in British Columbia, 1976—1980.* Vancouver, Pacific Association for Continuing Education, 1982.

Charner, Yvan. *Patterns of Adult Participation in Learning Activities.* Washington, D.C., National Institute for Work and Learning, 1980.

Clark, Ralph J.; Brundage, Donald. "Adult Education Opportunities in Canada, in Peterson, Richard E., et al., *Adult Education and Training in Industrialized Countries.* New York, Praeger, 1982, pp. 207—241.

Commission d'étude sur la formation des adultes, Montréal. *Apprendre: une action volontaire et responsable.* Québec, Ministère des Communications, 1982.

Commission of Inquiry on Educational Leave and Productivity, Ottawa. *Education and working Canadians.* Ottawa, labour Canada, June 1979.

Conférence des recteurs et des principaux des universités du Québec, Montréal. *Du collège à l'université: édition 1983—1984.* CREPUQ, 1983.

Council of Ministers of Education, Canada. *Aspects of Postsecondary Education in Canada.* Report prepared for OECD's Intergovernmental Conference on Policies for Higher Education in the 1980s. Toronto, CMEC, May 1981.

Council of Ministers of Education. *Postsecondary Education Issues in the 1980s.* Toronto, CMEC, 1983a.

Council of Ministers of Education. *Réponse à l'enquête de l'UNESCO sur le développement de l'éducation des adultes: avant projet.* Toronto, CMEC, 1983b.

Dandurand, Pierre; Fournier, Marcel. *Conditions de vie de la population étudiante universitaire québécoise.* Montréal, Université de Montréal, mai 1979.

Economic Council of Canada, Ottawa. *In Short Supply: Jobs and Skills in the 1980s.* ECC, 1982.

Federal Provincial Task Force on Student Assistance, Toronto. *Report.* Toronto, Council of Ministers of Education, — Ottawa, Secretary of State, 1981.

Forsythe, Kathleen; Collins, Valerie. *British Columbia Higher Education and the Integration of a New Technology (Case Study).* OECD-CMEC, November 1983.

Fortin, André, et al. *Collectivités et université: vers de nouveaux rapports.* Montréal, Université de Montréal, 1983.

Humphreys, Elizabeth; Porter, John. *Part-Time Studies and University Accessibility.* Ottawa,

Carleton University, October 1978.

Institut canadien d'éducation des adultes. *Adult Participation in Education and Training Leave Needs.* (translation) Montreal, ICEA, April, 1983.

Kaufman, David; Sweet, Robert. "Increased Educational Opportunity for Adults: A Canadian Example", *Higher Education* 8 (3) July—September, 1983, pp. 15—25.

Leslie, Peter M. *Canadian Universities 1980 and Beyond.* Ottawa, Association of Universities and Colleges of Canada, September 1980.

Ministère de l'Éducation (Ouébec). *Un projet d'éducation permanente: énoncé d'orientation et plan d'action en éducation des adultes.* Québec, 1984.

Ministère des Collèges et universités (Ontario). *Tour d'horizon: guide de l'éducation post-secondaire en Ontario 1984—1985.* Toronto.

National Advisory Panel on Skill Development Leave, Ottawa. *Learning for Life.* Ottawa, March 1984.

Ontario Ministry of Colleges and Universities. *Continuing Education in the Schools, Colleges and Universities of Ontario.* March 1983.

Ontario Ministry of Colleges and Universities. *Continuing Education: The Third System.* Toronto.

Ontario Ministry of Colleges and Universities. *Horizons 1984—85: A Guide to Post-Secondary Education in Ontario.* Toronto, March 1983.

Ontario Ministry of Colleges and Universities, Council of Ontario Universities, Ontario Council on University Affairs. *Interprovincial Comparisons of University Financing: Fifth Report of the Tripartite Committee on Interprovincial Comparisons.* January 1984.

Paquet, Pierre. *Le congé-éducation.* Montréal, Université de Montréal, mars 1983.

Paquet, Pierre. *Employer-Employee Interests in Job Training.* (Translation), Ottawa, Skill Development Leave Task Force, March 1983.

Paquet, Pierre; Doray, Pierre; Bouchard, Pierre. *Sondage sur les pratiques de formation en entreprise.* Quebec, Ministère des Communications, 1982.

Parliamentary Task Force on Employment Opportunities for the 80s. *Work for tomorrow: Employment Opportunities for the 80s.* Ottawa, 1981.

Peterson, Richard E., et al. *Adult Education and Training in Industrialized Countries.* New York, Praeger, 1982.

Ray, Douglas; Harley, Ann; Bayles, Michael. *Values, Life-Long Education and an Aging Canadian Population.* London, University of Western Ontario, 1981.

Revenue Canada, Ottawa. *Interpretation Bulleting IT-357R.* Ottawa, 1980.

Roberts, Hayden. *Culture and Adult Education.* Edmonton, University of Alberta, 1982.

Rubenson, Kjell. *Barriers to Participation in Adult Education.* Vancouver, University of British Columbia, 1983.

Secretary of State. *Guide to Federal Sources of Financial Aid.* Ottawa, Supply and Services, 1983a.

Secretary of State. *Support to Education by the Government of Canada.* Ottawa, Supply and Services, 1983b.

Simpson, Wayne. *An Economic Analysis of Industrial Training in Canada.* Ottawa, Economic Council of Canada, March 1983.

Skill Development Leave Task Force. *Learning a Living in Canada: Background and Perspectives.* Ottawa, Supply and Services Canada, 1983, vol. 1.

Skill Development Leave Task Force. *Learning a Living in Canada: Policy Options for the Nation.* Ottawa, Supply and Services Canada, 1983, vol. 2.

Social Program Evaluation Group. *A Study of Skill Development Leave Programs in Canadian Business and Industry.* Queen's University, Kingston, April 1983.

Statistics Canada, Ottawa. *Advance Statistics of Education (1985—86).* Ottawa, September 1985a (Catalogue 81—220).

Statistics Canada, Ottawa. *Continuing Education.* Ottawa, May 1978 (Catalogue 81—225 Annual), discontinued publication.

Statistics Canada, Ottawa. *Education in Canada: A Statistical Review for 1983—84*. Ottawa, July 1985b (Catalogue 81—229 Annual).

Statistics Canada, Ottawa. *Financial Statistics of Education (1981—82)*. Ottawa, December 1984a (Catalogue 81—208 Annual).

Statistics Canada. *Education Statistics Bulletin*, Ottawa, January 1985c, (Catalogue 81—002).

Statistics Canada. *Education Statistics Bulletin*, Ottawa, August 1985d, (Catalogue 81—002).

Statistics Canada. *Tuition and Living Accommodation Costs at Canadian Universities*. Ottawa, November 1983 (Catalogue 81—219 Annual).

Statistics Canada. *The Labour Force: January 1984*. Ottawa, February 1984b (Catalogue 71—001).

Statistics Canada. *Universities: Enrolment and Degrees (1983)*. Ottawa, September 1985e (Catalogue 81—204 Annual).

Task Force on Labour Market Development. *Labour Market Development in the 1980s*. Ottawa, CEIC, July 1981.

Thomas, Alan. *Adult Education and the Law*. Toronto, OISE, October 1983.

Thomas, Alan. *Learning in Society*. Ottawa, Canadian Commission for UNESCO. February 1983.

Thomas, Alan. *Skill Development Leave: Stages to Universal Access*. Toronto, Salasan Associates, March 1983.

Thomas, Alan, et al. *Labour Canada's Labour Education Program*. Ottawa, Labour Canada, 1982.

Thomas, Audrey M. *Adult Illiteracy in Canada: A Challenge*. Ottawa, Canadian Commission for UNESCO, 1983.

UNESCO. *Worldwide Inventory of Non-Traditional Post-Secondary Educational Institutions*. Paris, 1980.

Wainewicz, Ignacy. *Demand for Part-Time Learning in Ontario*. Toronto, OISE, 1976.

Zur-Muehlen, Max von. *Post and Present Graduation Trends at Canadian Universities and Implications for the Eighties with Special Emphasis on Women and on Science Graduates*. s.e., March 1982.